REEL OTTAWA

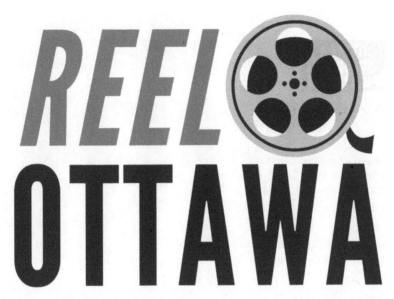

REEL OTTAWA

A MEMOIR

DAN LALANDE

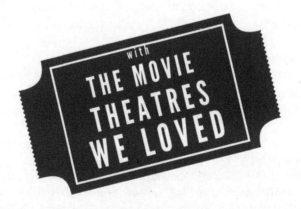

with THE MOVIE THEATRES WE LOVED

FOREWORD BY PHIL JENKINS

OTTAWA PRESS AND PUBLISHING

OTTAWA PRESS AND PUBLISHING

Ottawa Press and Publishing
ottawapressandpublishing.com

ISBN 978-1-988437-65-1 (softcover)
ISBN 978-1-988437-66-8 (epub)
ISBN 978-1-988437-67-5 (mobi)

Cover Design: Joanna D'Angelo
Interior Book Design/Formatting: Teri Barnett Indie Book Designer

Printed and Bound in Canada

Library and Archives Canada Cataloguing in Publication

Title: Reel Ottawa : a memoir / Dan Lalande ; foreword by Phil Jenkins.
Names: Lalande, Dan, author. | Jenkins, Phil, 1951- writer of foreword.

Identifiers: Canadiana (print) 20210181982 | Canadiana (ebook) 20210182121 | ISBN 9781988437651
(softcover) | ISBN 9781988437668 (EPUB) | ISBN 9781988437675 (Kindle)
Subjects: LCSH: Lalande, Dan. | LCSH: Motion picture theaters—Ontario—Ottawa—History. | LCSH: Screenwriters—Canada—Biography. | LCSH: Authors, Canadian—Biography. | LCGFT: Autobiographies.
Classification: LCC NA6846.C32 O885 2021 | DDC 725/.8230971384—dc23

To Nancy and Jessie, for the transition from reel to real.

CONTENTS

FOREWORD

For a brief, sweet eighteen months, I was a film critic. This was in the late 1970s, and a newly emerged Sunday Ottawa newspaper had, after I had successfully auditioned with reviews of a high-rise disaster movie and a Lassie musical, given me a get-into-the-movies-free card. For a hardcore film addict, it was a dream come true; I was being paid to watch and write about the movies. At the time there were over forty screens in Ottawa in which a fanatic such as I could spend my afternoons and evenings, three rows from the big light.

At the Oscars, there is a segment called In Memoriam, during which the names of those who have died are read out, engendering a feeling of loss. A similar feeling was evoked as I read *Reel Ottawa* and the roll call grew of theatres whose screens no longer shine. Rest in peace the Capitol, a true palace holding thousands, demolished in 1970; the Centre (later the Mall) on Sparks Street, where as a boy on his own I travelled to on the streetcar on Saturdays. And now the much-lamented Bytowne, shuttered in the time of Covid, wherein subtitles and singalongs were enjoyed.

The law of averages dictates that Dan Lalande and I must have been in one of those venerable Ottawa movie houses at the same time, at least once and probably many more times than that. Perhaps we were both in the Somerset when the announcement came that, "Anyone talking loudly during the movie will be escorted from the theatre and punished." Or maybe we were both appreciative of the tub of yogurt thrown at the screen in the Rideau when advertising, shown before the movie started, first polluted Ottawa's cinemas.

But those were minor movie moments. Could Dan have been one of the seven other people besides me in the huge St. Laurent Screen One when *The Matrix* had its first Ottawa run and, stunned, nobody got up to leave for several minutes, having spent two hours in a new, virtual world? Maybe he was one of those who applauded the screen in the Bytowne as the credits rolled on a cinema great, *Cinema Paradiso* or *Parasite*. I wish we had met back then (although we did later) in the Bytowne foyer to talk over each other about the latest foreign gem we had just relished.

Reel Ottawa rolls out in the series of vignettes, or scenes, or frames, that take Dan from his obsession at first sight to the film lover's inheritance he passes on to his daughter. As happens with a good book, it became weightless as I entered into it, just as the frame of the screen hosting a great movie disappears as it absorbs you.

There are many wonderful things about Dan's charming, moving, honest and humorous biography of his affair with celluloid. (Dan has written and performed comedy and posts daily wisecracks on social media; there is often a punch line at the end of his vignettes.) Primary is the acute self-awareness he brings to his evolution from boy in a family, to family man. Being a film fanatic shapes your life, and spills over into the lives of your nearest and dearest. The word pictures Dan creates of his often-fraught relationships with his parents, friends—best and otherwise—and his loving ones with his wife and child will generate echoes in many readers. They may well point them, as they did me, back to those movies whose themes were overlaps with their own emotional journey. For myself, father-and-son movies most of all.

The accumulated, sedentary thousands of hours Dan has spent immersed in larger-than-life stories have penetrated his personality. As with all of us hooked on movies, those hours spent on those secular places of worship infiltrate a moral code and form a self-image that the casual movie goer never experiences; and in my opinion is the lesser for it. Those silhouettes in the seats around you are your congregation, your tribe, your away-from Homies. The demi-gods of stardom and the auteurs of direction on display up on the screen are your role models. In *Reel Ottawa* movies as much as family maketh the man.

Reel Ottawa is also the chronicle of a day dreamer in pursuit of a dream come true. Movies are a form of daydream, in which you play a small but vital part, that of the watcher, the witness. There is a saying regarding travel that the person who leaves is not the person who returns. The same holds true for movies. You come out of the darkness into the real world moving from fiction into reality. But in some fractional way, you are not the same person who went in. The great scripts, directions, acting have beamed into you, and altered how you see the world. Repeat that process a hundred, a thousand, ten thousand times and you are, in part, as Dan is, what you have seen.

The dream of the lead actor in *Reel Ottawa,* Dan Lalande, is to someday write films; to produce scripts that, unlike most scripts, get made into movies, and see your name up there. That was Dan's dream, pretty well from the moment he first snuck into an Ottawa movie palace. I leave it to you to move from my cinematic musings into his story pages to discover if his dream came true. Lights, roll, action.

Phil Jenkins, Chelsea, Quebec,
March 2021

ACKNOWLEDGEMENTS

Foremost, a shout out to local hero Ron Corbett, who rescued this memoir from the nibbling of national interests and encouraged me, quite rightly, to make Ottawa a primary character.

Next, a great, big thanks to friend, editor, and cheerleader Joanna D'Angelo, for her encouragement, ideas, and great company.

To all of the family, friends, and acquaintances therein, for affording me a life as rich, complex, and enjoyable as any ever depicted onscreen.

Last but definitely not least, to those who owned, operated, and staffed Ottawa's movie theatres back in the proverbial day. Despite the usher's signature order "to please leave by the side entrance," some of us have stayed in perpetuity.

THE PREVIEW

THE HERO of John Cheever's celebrated short story *The Swimmer* figured out that the pools installed across his neighbourhood constituted, effectively, a river. By performing his morning strokes in each successive natatorium, he could navigate its entire length, finding himself, ultimately, back home.

It was years later, upon reading Cheever's melodramatic masterpiece for the umpteenth time, that I realized that I could do same, a hubristic round-trip not nautical but sentimental, visiting not pools but another recreational vehicle: movie theatres—specifically, Ottawa's, past and present (mostly, in our age of streaming, past). Inter alia, I'd reunite not with cocktail-swilling cohorts but with ghosts: family, friends, lovers held bittersweetly dear.

On nights when insomnia jostles me from bed, usually between three and four in the morning, I set out.

First, I stroll from my home in Old Ottawa South to the venerable Mayfair, the last local relic from the gilded age of moviegoing, still standing, miraculously, long after its rococo brothers—foremost, The Capitol—have passed. Within its mustily grandiose confines, I settle in, thin, bespectacled, all of twenty-one, alongside the girl, the first serious one in my life, awaiting me.

The tunes of the times—a lot of drum machine; this is the Eighties—taper. The house darkens, and we marvel at Marlon Brando and Maria Schneider in, a decade after its controversial release, *The Last Tango in Paris,* inspired by their ochre-coloured orgy into an animated episode of footsie, a child's version of what's progressing before us.

Moving on, I venture north on Bank Street, till it meets the crook where once stood The Somerset. The sizeable Somerset, with its expansive balcony, the only sensible vantage point from which to watch Lawrence trek Arabia, Gandhi incite India, or Darth Vader rule, aspirationally, outer space.

Further up, The Phoenix, the 1990's art house whose architectural pentimento is the notorious Rialto, where, as a boy, I am warned never to venture, regardless of how enticing, how affordable the films. Predators, it is rumoured, as well as toothy rats, permeate its elliptical shadows.

Even the equally inveigling arcade just up the way, at which the unshaven play pool, is of dubious reputation, its smell of steamed hot dogs and oily French fries the hot breath of the big, bad wolf. Soon, though, I will come of age and it, the theatre, will too, rising from the ashes as The Phoenix. There, another woman will await me: taller, more confident, fragrant. Improbably, she will become my wife. From our first apartment directly across the street, we will venture here, the site of our nervous first date, repeatedly, our post film discussions serving as foreplay as we return to our low-rent love shack.

From Centretown's apex, I cast an eye to my left, onto Queen. There, before the three-screen Capitol Square, my ne-er do well father and I seek refuge from an unrelenting snow, our noses red and drippy as we negotiate the box office before the salvific escalator ride to the promised land, where Jack Nicholson or Paul Newman or Barbra Streisand anticipate us, set to strengthen, through their onscreen tribulations, our bond.

Afterward, at the mercy of OC Transpo, Ottawa's notorious bus system (we don't have a car, nor much of anything, really) my dad, his heart bigger than his wallet (not hard), volunteers what is literally the last of our money, barring bus fare, to an inquiring derelict, who retreats into a drugstore to procure a thirst-quenching bottle of Aqua Velva. One night's pleasure deserves another, I guess my father philosophized.

Though I don't venture that way, past the Capitol Square stands, semi-hidden within the carapace of an office complex, the Place de Ville. The naughty *Blazing Saddles* (at least, naughty for its time, especially to a twelve-year-old) is playing. My Separatist grandfather, with his limited English, not only gets each ribald gag but laughs more heartily than most. Movies, I discover for the first time, aren't just movies. They're a lot of things, including, with *Pepère* as litmus, a barrier breaker, more effective and easier than the ones—confrontation, exasperation, reconciliation—offered by familial-political reality.

I round the mall to Elgin Street, home of downtown's flagship, the eponymous Elgin, the first, worldwide, to boast more than a single screen. I sit, self-pityingly, alone, and watch Jake LaMotta—Robert De Niro in macho clown mode—get mercilessly pummeled, over and over and over again, each blow a pattern, a repeated experience, as, once again, I have fallen (pre-wife) for the love of another man, suffering pang after pang after pang.

How to break free, as LaMotta-De Niro finally does, from fate's glove, how to get, behaviourially, from The Elgin to The Phoenix?

On the long, last leg of the journey, from Elgin to the Pretoria Bridge, from the scenic crannies of the leafy Glebe over yet another span, I know that, unlike Cheever's hero, I am not coming home to a life that has been shockingly shattering while I was obliviously self-occupied; that what awaits me is security; that happy endings—my wife, my child, my home—are not just kept in movie theatres past and present.

ACT ONE

I HAD no idea what to expect.

Only that in a few short moments, my mother, my grandmother, my sister and I—a quartet rarely formed—would stop rifling through racks of brightly coloured dresses and shelves of ivory-tone shoes and head off to something called a "movie theatre" (the Regent Theatre I discover years later, at the corner of Bank and Sparks).

I was about five. Any adventures I had had outside the house, my grandfather's two-story firetrap just off The LeBreton Flats, a French-English war zone in the working-class section of Ottawa, typically involved boisterous gangs of dust-decorated kids. We innocently staged battles against one another in the sand pits behind the buildings or floated plastic boats in a tin tub periodically arranged for us by the adults, desperate to engineer a more peaceful, and cleaner, form of play.

We entered. Oppressive darkness, Old World decor. I felt both suffocated and comforted.

Suddenly, a soft whirr pierced the spooky-cosy placidity, cuing an ambitious beacon of off-yellow light. Seconds later, great swaths of colour danced funnily before me, to tinny, archaic interludes of music and the odd snatches of arch, snappy dialogue. Soon, these sensorial stimulations began to synchronize into a story: the curious tale of a black-haired beauty and her seven funny friends.

The sequence that imprinted itself on me most took place in a diamond mine. That, I learned, was where short, cherubic people spent their days, before retreating to the communal cottages that they called home.

Different as they were from anyone in the world in which I lived, I nevertheless began to wonder whether what I was seeing was a viable sub-world operating just outside of mine, a world my parents simply hadn't gotten around to telling me about yet.

Oh yes, they'd someday announce, we meant to tell you: there are fun-loving cherubs with big, rosy noses, some who speak and some who don't. They live in the woods not far from *Pepère*'s, the ones you're not allowed to play in.

When the Wicked Queen converted herself into an unforgettably decrepit crone, I knew, somehow, that this conversation between my parents and I was never going to take place. Whatever I was seeing, I realized, was something that existed entirely for its own sake, not an alternate reality but something else, something that enriched and reframed ours.

Further, judging by everyone's heightened emotional subscription, that it was something that we all, for whatever reasons, periodically appeared to require, with the same sense of need Snow White had for the love and support of the dwarves or the magic kiss of the prince who sang instead of talked.

When we finally emerged into the blinding sunlight, the rush for the bus and the familiar chatter about dinner affirmed that indeed, there was but one world.

Still, I knew now that it had woods, the kind, albeit virtual, that were safe for me to get lost in.

☆☆☆☆☆

THEY WERE as much rivals as siblings, each desperate for the approval of their taciturn father, the man whose wife had left him shortly after birthing four children, including the book ends, the eldest and the youngest, the sisters.

He was everything to those girls, regardless of his lukewarm responses to their needs: their solvency, their connection, the thin string that prevented them from being set adrift, orphans in a big, bad world.

And big and bad it was: the aforementioned LeBreton Flats, twinned to boot with Preston Street, where the Italians were quick to respond, fists flailing, to the jibes of the native-born. Together, this small, central section of the city boasted an eclectic, volatile *dramatis personae:* drunken war veterans, Andy Capp-style husbands and wives, iconic 50's toughs—some of whom went on to become the most notorious criminals in the country.

The brothers, they reveled in it. It was their anchor, their substitute for the sense of connection the old man couldn't offer. But that same world would have swallowed those little girls whole—so they sought refuge in the only symbol of security, such as it was, that they knew.

I wasn't aware of that dynamic at the time, of course, all of this rivalry for that dilapidated house's one precious commodity. But I was getting my first glimpse of it, as I sat between my mother and her sister and watched the first ever TV broadcast of *Whatever Happened to Baby Jane*.

They took such interest in the friction between the characters, Gothic apple doll Bette Davis and simmering, sunken-eyed Joan Crawford. They would make comments, have small, heated exchanges about which character's behavior was warranted and which wasn't, and, whenever they took time out from this taut two-hander for a taut two-hander of their own, would check up on how I was handling the film. Even that they fought about.

I, of course, being extremely young, had no idea—just as they, for different reasons, had no idea—that a twin agenda was at work. It would not be until years later that I would experience the Freudian flash that would equate the onscreen with the off.

In the film, the rivalry is resolved with the death of one of the sisters. It's possible that that's exactly what happened in real life: my mother died a few short years ago, and her sister, long estranged, surprised us all by appearing at the funeral.

So, rivalry resolved there too. Cue Bette Davis, obliviously dancing in the film's final frames.

☆☆☆☆☆

HE WOULD EAT the soup as fast as he could, before the next wave would upset the balance of the ship, sending the bowl back across the table to its rightful owner. Another whoosh, another tilt, and the soup would be right back in front of him, his for the contraband consumption.

As he gobbled hurriedly, we all laughed, that ear-piercing scream-like laugh only kids in spiritual synchronicity can produce. There we were, frog-like on our blue and white floor cushions, eyes fixated on the smallish screen, faux Dick-And-Jane white picket fence corralling us from the mob milling at the mall.

We had just moved, my parents, my sister and I, to this urban wonderland, had just made the all-saving transition—at my protective father's insistence—from the rough'n'tumble Flats to this placid, plastic land far, far away: Montreal's gleaming West Island.

My sister and I spent our first days marveling over the size of our new house (albeit modest to most) that was suddenly, improbably ours. We gazed agape too at the village's storybook main drag: a bank, a grocer's, a stationary store. And the neighbourhood kids: well-scrubbed, well-meaning, and, unless seriously provoked, well-mannered.

We picked shad flies off of shop windows and admonished anyone whose dog would dare relieve itself against the stop signs or the telephone poles. Nothing, if we could help it, would be sullied. This precious chance at a decent existence we had been handed, this small, welcome miracle, had to be preserved in all its glory.

Over the coming days, like kids in a candy shop (there was even one of those—and a place that made pizza!) we watched our mom prettify herself at the local beauty parlour, bought comic books whenever our school marks earned dad's pocket change, and spent hour upon hour at the park, which—get this! —had *two* sets of swings, *two* giant slides, and, way at the back, a *swimming pool*.

Then, there was the jewel in the crown: the mall, with ornate fountains that lit up poetically pink and baby blue, its beckoning stores stocked with shiny plastic toys, and its myriad places to eat, featuring such exotic fare as burgers made with steak and sandwiches, of a sort, made with ice cream. If you were particularly well behaved, you left this consumerist paradise with a bright yellow balloon, a Pez dispenser of Baloo the Bear or Zorro, or a silvery new cap gun.

Once, Batman, then all the rage on television, even showed up. *Batman!* He brought Robin with him of course. They both emerged from the gleaming black Batmobile. They looked curiously fatter than on TV and spoke with French Canadian accents. One of them, mysteriously, smelled of something that hurt your eyes when he breathed (maybe to ward off The Joker?) But it had to be them. This was the mall, after all, that place where all things were possible—besides, they had the car. They signed our hands. None of us washed until our parents, about a week or so later, absolutely insisted.

Then, just when venturing there began to venture on routine, the white picket fence was set up, the one guarding the floor cushions, upon which our parents demanded we sit while they disappeared. Again, as in the *Snow White* experience, I heard that goose-pimple producing hum, as it introduced that ever promising cone of light. This time, though, replacing the uninteresting white rectangle before me was a small, sad-eyed man in shabby clothing, sneakily sipping soup to plain, plinky piano music.

If we, the gathered, were to understand the odd bits of writing that took him away from us a little too often, this tiny, rumpled creature was on his way from a world of poverty to one populated with promise—a journey not too far removed from the one my family and I had just made.

Though he was definitely distinct from Dopey, this funny little person too didn't speak, and like that most lovable of the dwarves, his entire mode of survival seemed to be the ability to be cute. Charlie Chaplin in *The Immigrant*, I remembered some opening words telling me...but there were no closing words to tell me whether or not, at the end, he ever got to where he was going.

Nevertheless, I knew—I knew that he had found paradise.

After all, one such as I was there, wasn't I?

☆☆☆☆☆

"OH DANNY BOYYYY...THE pipes, the pipes are caaaallingggg..."

I cannot hear one bar of that iconically Irish ditty without it being in his soft, accommodating lilt.

It was, in effect, their doorbell, the sound their house made whenever I approached, from mine across the street. And though these homes were but a few feet away from one another, they were worlds apart.

Theirs was larger, smelled of fatty foods we never ate, and featured a large, homey addition suggesting another time: a spacious Victorian back room, complete with that most cliché of 19th century commodities, a perpetually blazing hearth (even, if memory serves, in summer!)

And the downstairs was divided into several interesting areas: a sauna, a spare bedroom featuring a colour TV (still a rich man's plaything), and a red carpeted parlour reeking of Guinness, its centrepiece an acre-long pool table.

Though we never played pool, my best friend and I, we spent countless hours at that table. There, we improvised a game in which, by hand, one pool ball was sent on a horizontal journey from side pocket to side pocket, while another, from the opposite end of the table, was sent gunning for it.

The exterior of this spacious property was surrounded by a section of apple trees (dangerously, we would plunge the ends of our Daisy air rifles into the fallen fruit, point our barrels at one another and shoot) and their novel cousins (at least for Eastern Canada), trees that bore pears and plums!

At lunch, over hot dogs (always hot dogs), we would burn our initials or those of any girls we had developed an eye for into a picnic table, courtesy of our Cracker Jack box-supplied magnifying glasses, while the skull of a long horned cow—that's correct—kept a creepy eyehole on us (it was one of the many curios that belonged to his older brother, who, in that complicated era—the '60's—had mysteriously left home, his things—including an old pump organ—having been too difficult to bring along).

All of this was made normal by his father, a rumpled, adorable Irishman who loved to sing me *Danny Boy*, his class-conscious but accepting mother (who took me into the fold despite her pseudo-English reservations) and his lively sisters, whom I never ceased to naturally amuse with my self-deprecating, if often accidental, wit.

When not playing our yet to be patented pool ball game or attempting to take each other's eyes out with fruit, my BFF and I could be found in the spare bedroom, our guns carefully aimed at the largest of the house's many TVs, on the lookout for any anonymous, blonde-haired actor wearing a Nazi uniform. At the first sight of him, our mouths would reel off endless streams of amateurish sound effects, simulating the firing of our weapons.

By the end of each film, we were proud comrades in arms with whichever square jawed hero—from John Garfield to Errol Flynn to John Wayne—we had decided to join up with.

No doubt that sight was one of the things that had made his father, who had grown up in Hitler's Europe (even if Ireland) sing so sweetly to me.

☆☆☆☆☆

THEY DID THINGS. They went away on weekends, traveled to Europe, and almost weekly it seemed, ventured, *en famille*, to the movies. When I was lucky, I'd just happened to be playing with their youngest when everyone was rounded up for just such an excursion, off to watch whatever was *de rigueur*. Often, my best friend would protest; he'd rather spend that time with me, he'd whine, aiming our war toys at TV Germans. These cries of his were always a marvel to me—how could anybody balk at a trip to the movies?

We, on the other hand, never attended. Never. Only many years later, during a brief but sadly unsuccessful reconciliation between my now divorced parents, did we ever find ourselves as one in a movie theatre. What idyllic days! If I'm romantic about the movies, it's no doubt because they are tied-in to that brief, magical period, with its promise of life working out movie-style: my parents, after an acrimonious divide, miraculously fused together again. But life is not the movies. That exuberant period lasted but a half-dozen films. Mom went on to a second marriage, dad to a long and difficult soul-search.

All I went away with, in the end, was self-pity, a tortuous, alienating characteristic that defined me well into my late twenties. Most of my inner life was taken up by the ridiculous wish that I could go back and rewrite my early years, that I could make my family our neighbours: happy, outgoing, and—the thing it took me years to figure out that they were and we weren't—solvent.

I was twenty-two, I think, when it finally occurred to me that all of those tall tales my parents recounted about their upbringing, amongst shell-shocked drunkards, battling couples, and James Dean-style baddies, were not products of their imagination, cooked up, movie-style, for the amusement of my sister and me. By repeatedly imparting them like bedtime stories, they were setting the seeds for an eventual epiphany: why our neighbours went to things like the honorary-Oscar-fueled Charlie Chaplin revival of 1972 and we didn't.

I've since seen all of those Chaplin films, of course, countless times. I've shared them with friends, girlfriends, a wife, a daughter, without once suffering a retroactive pang of class division—with one exception...

The last close up of *City Lights*. In Charlie's loving apologia of a face, spawned by the blind girl's realization that he is not the well-to-do man she has mistaken him for, I see my parents, no strangers to tramp-style circumstance, and the poetry of the deception they knew their children would someday uncover.

✰✰✰✰✰

SHE ATTENDED REGULARLY, often dragging her younger brother—my best friend—with her, or her giddy girlfriends. She would come home after these excursions and recruit us—the neighbourhood kids, all younger—into the kind of play that offered a living précis of what she had just seen, with her, of course, as the heroine.

She would sing—a la Liza—do comedy—a la Goldie—or vamp—a la Raquel. The object of her affection in these impromptu performances was, for reasons I never entirely figured out, me.

My still-developing loins would surge with each wily purr,

each catty come-on, each doe eyed mug. The other kids usually giggled over these amateurish reactions—as a fellow player, I was definitely not in her league—or at the crimson colour that my face took on whenever she poured it on too thick.

The whole thing would end, always, with her laughing, reverting to her normal self, then bidding us goodbye—off to her real life, brother in tow, across the street.

I, too, would pack up my "actor's trunk" and again become the anonymous ten-year old who played with cars, struggled with homework, and hung out at the park.

But a conspiracy of precedents, unbeknownst to my young self, was being deeply imprinted by these star turns of hers: an appreciation for just how personal one's relationship with film could be. And—all art aside—an infatuation with that species known as the older woman, a Freudian residue that would lead me to sabotage relationships with partners my own age in favour of the wiser, the more mature, and—in too many cases—the taken. I gave up hills in favour of mountains, locking myself repeatedly into a series of exhausting climbs; an endless game of emotional catch-up, all in an effort to play on par with the elusive older sister of my then best friend.

Though I lost touch with that family many years ago, after the move prompted by the break-up of my parents, I still find myself thinking of them, and in particular, her. She is dancing dramatically around the slim trio of poplar trees that were the centrepiece of our yard, as Liza, Goldie or Raquel, a song or joke on her lips, setting herself free while chaining others.

☆☆☆☆☆

THE SQUEAKY BONK THE PLASTIC, oversized carrot with the smiley face on it made was the first word, in effect, I ever said to him. The first he ever said to me came in the form of a long, loud wail, enough to rattle the windows of every home in the 'hood. We all laughed at this—myself and the slightly older kids I had managed to impress with my half-hearted torture of this pint-sized newcomer—as we watched him peddle off, still crying, the carrot ironically smiling back from the wagon hitched to his retreating tricycle.

Other types of taunts, as we aged, followed, like pointing out that he was never brought to the movies (not that any of us, my BFF aside, were taken very often). Being younger, and having those mysteriously moody parents to boot, it would take a lot more begging on his part to get to see things with guns and cars and girls. So, whenever we were able to go and he wasn't, we rubbed it, endlessly it seemed, into his little crying face.

Then came that afternoon in his garage. None of us saw it but somehow, we all heard about it: the occasion on which his father attacked his mother, and his mother implored him to grab a snow shovel—the nearest damaging object, I suppose—with which to hit his father, so that his father would stop hitting his mother.

I'm sure it created a dark, deep hole inside him, one he went on feeling for a long, long time. I'd like to think that as he grew—we lost contact before I turned thirteen—he flirted with replicating his father's behaviour, realized he had a problem, and sought help. I'd also like to think that he is now a model human being, kind and appreciative, with a loving, respectful relationship with his wife, his children, and the world.

Then again, maybe I've seen too many movies.

☆☆☆☆☆

HAD I been old enough to have seen the film, I would have made the comparison instantly.

There he stood, lording over us from atop his early-morning perch, the giant, concrete balustrade separating the steps into the school from its vast courtyard. We were lined up before him like troops awaiting inspection.

Every morning we endured this ritual, from kindergarten through to grade six; our principal, in life a bald, old fashioned, unimpressive man, presented to us as a figure to be admired, as a voice, literally, from on high, as the ultimate authority on all—as it was a strict Catholic school, let's say it: as God.

Patton, that's the film, had we been old enough to see it, his daily speeches would have constantly conjured. We were the anonymous military entity George C. Scott, by way of our black-suited principal, had so emphatically and colourfully addressed.

This general's speeches, however, unlike his big screen avatar's, became tired fast: school announcements, behavioural protocol, and, inevitably, one's duty to the Christian deity. But there was always, somewhere in his straight and narrow, a small left turn, a touch of the idiosyncratic: in most cases, a mention of the movies.

Mixed in with this ritualistic attempt to keep us in line was, more often than not, a recommendation. They were almost never kids' films, or family films, as those kinds of things in that era—the late Sixties and early Seventies—were in increasingly short supply. They were films he would urge us to go and tell our parents to see, often with the same stern and urgent tone he would apply to a direct order, like getting your report card signed or getting you to remind your family that Wednesday was Vaccine Day. If the film he had caught that week had left a particularly large mark on him, he would take the time—though we might be standing in a snowdrift even—to paint some of its more colourful scenes, hands gesticulating poetically as he recreated choice moments from grand, adult entertainments such as *Young Winston, Waterloo* or *West World.*

Inside a lot of us was a half-formed quest for the man's motives.

He was trying to make himself less frightening to us maybe,

more human; I wondered sometimes if that, sneakily, was his game; that he wanted us to think of him, definitely, as a figure to be obeyed but too as somebody approachable; the kind of avuncular character who might strike up a conversation, about the movies let's say, with your parents, or take them out one night, along with his wife, to the Alexis Nihon.

Then again, there was the chance he was less strategically minded. Perhaps it was simply that he was French—it was a French school—and that film, as both the Parisians and the Quebecois have ably demonstrated, is an inherent part of the French soul, a part not, even above one's duty, to be suppressed.

Or it could be that the guy was a film nut plain and simple, and like all film nuts, could not help but go on ad nauseam about the movies that had so enervated him, regardless of how incongruous or indifferent the audience.

I never found out.

A few short years ago, while attending a wedding, I met the man's spitting image. It was—surprise!—his twin brother, a relation I never knew existed. We spoke briefly, then I asked him how his brother was doing.

"Not well. About all he can do now is watch movies."

My broad smile baffled him.

☆☆☆☆☆

I SET the alarm for two A.M.

I had to see them, in the same manner that just a few short years earlier, I had to stay up and see Santa Claus.

I had to know that they existed, that they weren't just enthusiastic rantings of my father's; that indeed, at one point in time, and alive still through television, three crazy brothers, each with a distinct, exaggerated look and talent, disrupted the haughtily humdrum with the most unconventional of behaviours.

That they should subscribe to the way that we, children, did things well into their adult years gave me hope—hope that maybe conformity wasn't waiting to rob me of my energy, my uniqueness, my funniness. That one could be a kid forever.

But the alarm never got the chance to wake me from my sleep. Long before the fateful hour approached—why oh why were they airing this movie at two A.M? On a school night no less?—I was up, too thrilled with the prospect to catch so much as a wink.

To the living room I tiptoed, thinking that I'd bide my time with something banal before the feature.

What I caught instead fired me up as much, I was sure, as the much anticipated first glimpse of the Marx Brothers would.

Gary Cooper and company in *Beau Geste*: adventure, gun play, camaraderie.

Did the black and white world of which I had heard so much really hold that much excitement, enough to contain a subworld such as this *plus* the Marxes?

By the time *Duck Soup* aired, I was completely beside myself! It was all I could do to jump up and down on the couch, muffling each laugh or squeal of delight with a pillow, hoping beyond hope that I wouldn't wake them, my mother and stepfather, neither of whom would appreciate my late night, contraband visit to this life-altering alternate universe.

Around four, to bed I went—again unable to sleep, mixes of both films, bullets and bon mots, replaying in my mind like a projector in perpetual motion.

In the morning, after a modicum of sleep, I awoke—bleary eyed, off kilter, miserable.

There was but one world for me now, and this—with its stern, inquisitive faces staring back at me suspiciously over the breakfast table—was not the one.

✰✰✰✰✰

COWARDICE.

That's what it was, that magic quality that made them different from you and me, that gave them their childlike energy, their poetic, high-speed physicality, their capacity for witticism.

To a man—I use that term loosely—they exhibited it: Danny Kaye, darting about a boxing ring on misshapen legs; Bob Hope, donning disguises and desperately dodging demise; Lou Costello, able to face the real world only at the bellicose bullying of his fair-weather bud Bud.

We traded their escapades in the schoolyard, just the way we traded sports cards or gossip about girls. Did you see the part where...? I liked it when...The best part definitely was...

And if you were fortunate enough to catch them not in prime time but on a school day afternoon, when you were at home sick, you were the envy of your peers—for you, and only you, had had an audience with a deity.

Early one weekday morning, as the snowballs began to fly—the English, on their way to school, against we French, waiting at the bus stop—I decided to slip into the jaundiced skin that was the team jacket of filmdom's funnymen.

All the while, the battle intensified, projectiles peppering the air. In true Canadian tradition, the French fought valiantly but in the end, lost. They were short one man. He was hiding around the corner, giddy with anticipation for the laugh he would get when his humble, cowardly presence, Bob Hope-style, would emerge with a Lou Costello bounce to utter the Danny Kaye-worthy, "H-h-have they left yet?"

So great would the ensuing roar be, he was certain, that in true comic movie fashion, the snow that was piled up on the roof above his friends would shake from appreciative laughter. Then, as the last, unseen enemy, snowball in hand, attempted to sneak up on one of them, down upon his unsuspecting head would come the decisive hundred pounds of snow—the coward, as always, accidentally saving the day.

There was no such victory of course, for there was no such laugh. Instead, stunned silence.

From that moment until the end of childhood, there was only one social caste with which I would feel comfortable: the coward class—Danny, Bob and Lou—from whom I could learn, I hoped, how to win acceptance through inadequacy.

★★★★★

HE ALWAYS FELT that he had given away too much of himself in it, that if he'd had the chance to do it again—as if any of his scenes in *The Last Tango in Paris* needed a retake!—he would revert to what he had been doing for years: fooling people, guarding his innermost pain by way of tall tales, oblique remarks, and dark, often cruel humour.

All of these are in *Tango* too, of course, but presented willy-nilly, between the boundary-crossing true confessions.

Brando at his purest is in the scene where, toying with a harmonica, he recreates a real-life experience from his Nebraska upbringing. It's evident in the telling that he still feels the humiliation he suffered that fateful day when he took out a prize prospect, unaware that he had cow shit on his shoes.

Had it been me instead of Brando in that film, I know exactly what story I would have recounted. It's nowhere near as dramatic or memorable but it conjures in me, even to this day, the same prickly personal pang that the cow shit story evoked in him.

We are not in Nebraska anymore. We are in suburban Montreal, mid-winter. A kid brings some object or other into my Grade Four class—I couldn't even tell you what, only that it impresses both the hard-to-please teacher and my equally hard-to-please classmates.

Determined to do same, I spread a rumor during recess that I, too, will be bringing a major surprise for the class this week. I can already see the delighted expressions on the faces of both my teacher and my peers as she unveils the thing that will make me the newly gilded Golden Boy: a gleaming new fishbowl for the class fish (somehow, my family has a spare).

Instead, I get an unwelcome lesson in the delicate nature of audience expectation. All through the remainder of the day, at intervals of every few seconds it seems, classmates of all stripes are sharing their unreasonably high expectations with me: is it candy for the entire class? Is it new set of puppets, inspiring our teacher to forgo school work for an impromptu puppet show? Is it an expensive new model airplane all the boys will be put to work on?

The next morning, my family's spare fishbowl in tow, I begin to cross the mile-high snow that is my yard. Halfway across, I look down upon the bowl. Suddenly, I note its emptiness, and in that emptiness, I see the emptiness of my classmates, expecting more…much more.

Deciding that the taunts the empty-handed might receive are prospectively less painful than the ones directed at those who cast swine before pearls, I decide that I must get rid of this thing. Rather than bring it back home and be forced to explain my stirrings to my mother, I bury it deep in the snow.

My home-made mittens scraping hard against our yard's top layer is the sound of Brando's shoes as they are set free from the cow shit.

✯✯✯✯✯

HIS HAIRY, elongated likeness had been captured by a shakily held Bell and Howell—the shakes the result, one presumed, of irrepressible fear. Those few, faultily filmed frames came at you at unrelenting intervals, the caulking in every commercial-sized crack in favourite sitcoms, cartoon shows, and other Grade School media staples.

Conforming as it did to best (if unscrupulous) toy-selling practice, the result, expectedly, was the same: continuous cries by overstimulated grade-schoolers of *I want it!* or, in this case, *I want to see it!*

Who I talked into taking me and my companions to the movie theatre to see this monstrosity—given the nature of the film, a faux documentary cashing in on the Sasquatch-spotting craze, a monstrosity *within* a monstrosity—I don't remember. Even the film, save for the original image provided by the relentlessly played ad, I don't remember.

What I do remember is the drive home.

Debating some of the "facts" that the film had presented to us, I caught a glimpse over one of my backseat buddies' shoulders: there, in a park in which we regularly played on swings, climbed the monkey bars, and enjoyed other innocent pastimes, was a soldier—an actual, fatigue-fitted, walkie-talkie talking soldier. Needless to say, the incongruity of this—this was suburban Montreal, after all—struck me harder than that first glimpse of that half man-half ape from the film we had just seen.

Over the next few days, I received, piecemeal, something that the film could not, despite best efforts, provide: a plausible explanation for a mysterious and frightening apparition. Curiously, it was all of three letters—FLQ—and yet over the next few days, that small section of the alphabet would begin to strike more and more terror into the hearts of those around me.

So maybe, as my father had contended after I had attempted to share some of the more persuasive bits of that supposed documentary with him, there was no Sasquatch.

But irrefutably, there were monsters.

✯✯✯✯✯

"Just throw me the ball," I begged. "Make it look like an accident."

And so, he did—the biggest, most obvious violation of character imaginable.

The other kids in the schoolyard—those on the other side of the well-worn painted line, now scrambling to get away from me as, armed with his mistake, I neared—groaned about the size of the gaff for what seemed like an hour, switching to gales of derogatory laughter when my shot, predictably, missed every one of them.

The schoolyard game of dodgeball went on, with my friend getting his hands on the ball again and soon doing what he always did: knocking off members of the opposing team, my team, one by one, without one of us ever being able to catch any of his rocket-hard throws and take our turn at eliminating the competition.

He was black-haired, muscular—surprisingly so for a preteen—and above all, cool. He had no problem with girls, academia, or sports, particularly sports.

What he had a problem with was his father.

His father was a nerdy, old-fashioned kind of man (my friend's tough-guy looks came from God knew where), always dressed in a plain white shirt and heavy horn-rimmed glasses that had gone out of a fashion a few years before. Almost everything about him, in fact, suggested a soft-toned introvert. But left a little room, he could opine loudly, moodily, and definitively. In short, his accountant's exterior caged a vociferous brute.

One Sunday, another dodgeball game looming in the morning, we decided to go to the movies: *McQ*, John Wayne's foray into the vigilante cop genre that had become the rage with the successes of *Billy Jack*, *Walking Tall* and *Death Wish*. It was playing at the nearest theatre, in the shadow of our much-loved mall.

Finally! we sighed. We had had more than our fill of Disney;

here was a movie tailor-made for pre-teen males, promising brutality, bullets, and blood. We were thrilled!

And thrilled, after the movie, we remained. We liked it so much, particularly the climactic chase scene on the beach, we had decided to stay for another showing...unaware that my friend's tougher-than-John-Wayne father had decided to pick us up after the first show, and that he had been sitting in the family car, idling, for close to two hours already.

With the discovery of this intimidating fact—through a phone call to my friend's mother after showing Number Two—I saw my best friend shrink impossibly to just another ordinary twelve-year old.

Back at his house, I watched, silently stunned, as the toughest, coolest, most untouchable character I had ever known, was beaten, literally, to tears—a voluminous cascade, in fact, the duration of which I could never have imagined anyone letting forth, particularly him.

"You can't tell anybody about this!" he begged me afterwards. "Tell me that you won't. Tell me! *Tell me!!!*"

Okay then.

A ball for a bawl.

☆☆☆☆☆

I HAD CONVINCED HIM, despite the fact that I was twelve, that I was a bona fide member of this fast-moving fraternity; that somewhere, somehow, outside of the weighty, all-consuming responsibilities of Grade Six, playground time, and the dictates of my parents, I was a spy, secretly enjoying gun-blazing, hormone-charged, death-defying adventures a la James Bond.

As proof, I offered pictures of my superiors—those stuffy, pipe smoking Colonial leftovers who, with dour deadpan, set we smarmy, wise-cracking secret agents straight. They reminded us of the genuine dangers of our jobs, and, replacing their stuffy demeanor for a moment with grandfatherly regard, warned us, vainly, to be careful.

I frantically searched the house. Surely there was a photo of an uncle, a distant relation, a faraway family friend who might fit the bill; someone in a suit, at an occasion other than a graduation or a wedding, at the ready to save me from exposure as the misguided, starry-eyed phony that I was.

Nothing.

Desperate, I settled for whatever I could find: pictures of my estranged father. I hadn't seen him, due to my parents' recent divorce (dad had moved back to Ottawa; mom hadn't yet but would) for some time. How could this boy, whom I prided myself so much on bringing this far into my ruse, possibly check?

Dad looked almost convincing: no suit or jacket, no pipe or particularly stern face but a smile that was at least reluctant and a turtleneck that could definitely pass for stuffily old school.

Suddenly, like a prying agent attuned to the remotest footsteps of an approaching interloper, I sensed my schoolmate. A quick look out the window confirmed my well-trained suspicions. This was it. I would have to convince him with this photo or face the shattering fact, delivered to the smartest kid in school no less, that I did not belong to a world any more exciting, romantic or better than the one in which I lived, broken family, mediocre school life and all.

"You got it?" he asked, a fellow spy prompting a secret exchange.

"Of course," I answered just as coolly.

He stared at the photograph, then back up at me.

"Funny," he finally offered. "I can't help but see a resemblance between you and your boss."

It was not my father he had just set eyes on. Something had prevented me from going through with my plan. Dad was too sacred a thing to trifle with, too precious a commodity to use, the way, say, mom did with her derogatory barbs. I would spare my father, who had suffered so much, any further disservices.

It was my school picture from last year—a version hastily altered by a brown magic marker, in which, hurriedly, I had drawn an utterly unconvincing mustache.

An explosion. Laughter. Mine. I made it long and loud; after all, I now had to convince him that the whole thing had been a perfect set-up from the get-go.

"I can't believe I got you! *You! You!*"

His embarrassed giggling affirmed the success of my deception about my deception. I had done it after all. I had outsmarted a force more intelligent and powerful than mine.

Just like James Bond.

☆☆☆☆☆

I COULD SEE her out of the corner of my eye, lying still in her white bedroom—dreaming, I hoped? In silent agony, perhaps? ...or, God forbid, lifeless?

I couldn't tell. Not even the low-voiced mutterings of my stepfather (mom had hastily remarried) which in that surreal moment, my head spinning, I was barely paying attention to, were succeeding in letting me know exactly what was going on. Something, I seem to recall, about liquor and a prescription...or was it just the prescription?

I knew she'd been depressed, certainly; I was all of thirteen but I knew *that,* that something very major, and very adult, had been grinding away inside of her for some time.

There was that sunny summer afternoon, for instance, when I emerged from an energetic dip in our apartment complex's swimming pool to find that while she had been sitting there sunning herself, she had been crying. Tears were streaming down her face wetter and fatter than the chlorine infused ones falling off my emaciated frame.

"Mom…what's wrong?"

She sputtered, her face reddened…finally, she came out with something.

"Your uncle." Her younger brother. The hippie. "He's dead."

I told her that I understood, then escaped as quickly as possible into the pool, back into the wild, noisy, overcrowded world of childhood, grateful to eclipse a more complicated universe.

A few short years later, we all bumped into her happy, healthy younger brother. I lovingly said nothing…but my mind immediately flashed back to that surreal afternoon, and then, to that occasion in the bedroom.

In that moment, my soul ached for the presence of good-hearted Jack Lemmon, the heroic schmuck from that old black and white movie I had sneakily caught on television one night, *The Apartment*, to try his charming best to revive her, the way he had poor Shirley MacLaine.

Like Shirley, I would discover years later, my mother had been suffering from serious romantic malaise. Letters written to my father, from whom she had been divorced less than a year at the time, would tell me so. That trying state, caught between husbands old and new, was tearing her apart, she wrote, perhaps even…killing her.

I can't remember how the climax of this inner torment of hers was dealt with. My guess is that an ambulance came, and that my mother was brought to hospital.

All I can tell you is that a few days later, life was, unbelievably, back to its familiar rhythms. Mom was making breakfasts, going to work, dealing with her current husband.

Her thoughts, though, must have constantly been entertaining the proverbial road not taken—life in a renewed relationship with my father—the same way that mine, whenever I again caught her in moments of private, silent sadness or of uncle-caliber lies, kept returning to sweet, despondent Shirley MacLaine, doing her best in an unworthy alternate ending.

✰✰✰✰✰

SHE TALKED ABOUT THE MOVIES, an indulgence her orphan's home upbringing ill afforded, with giddy delight, though she ventured to them little. For one, she was ailing now, in more and more places each day. For another, the theatres were a considerable distance away, and there was the television, which provided most of the genre of thing she liked: comfortably paced, adequately spirited, humourous but not hilarious.

Each exuded an old-fashioned aura of simplicity, gentility, and unforced comfort—the components of the vibe she always, even in her longest moments of self-pity, gave off.

Come Christmas, though, a film came to theatres in just said mode. Off she prompted us—my father, now located back in Ottawa, and my sister, and I, visiting—through an unforeseen assault of snow to the prestigious Elgin, downtown Ottawa's flagship theatre, to watch Walter Matthau and George Burns lightly rival as *The Sunshine Boys*. The characters were her age (even if Matthau's years were make-up), the jokes were her level, and the spirit, for all of the verbal volleying, hers too.

As my father's mother (*Memère*, we called her) delighted in the film, we, in turn, delighted in her, losing ourselves in each one of her endorsing smiles, polite laughs, and sympathetic sneers. For a stretch, she was a girl again, that orphan girl, rescued by lightness from the daunting dark.

We exited. By now, the snowfall was unmerciful—but to a person, we afforded it no seriousness.

After all, it had just been proven that heavier skies could be lifted.

✯✯✯✯✯

ANY EDITOR WORTH his hard-working eyes would balk at the burden of the following crosscut: *A Thousand Clowns* and *Ordinary People*. And yet, these tectonic cinematic plates would create the perfect patchwork by which to represent my adolescence.

Half of it was spent with my father, in a low-rent, Alta Vista apartment complex, the stage for exhibitions of his humanely philosophical wit. The other half was spent in the company of my remade mother—in another Ottawa suburb: Gloucester—whose second marriage and career success had created an atmosphere of fragile propriety.

After their dramatic break-up and their marriage's failed sequel, my parents found themselves, as I've mentioned, back home. Not only at opposite ends of the city but at opposite ends of the social spectrum: dad unemployed and in a state of deep personal reflection, mom well-to-do and at a wobbly but welcome peace.

Back and forth I shuttled, a practice dictated by my need *du jour*. If it was spiritual or intellectual stimulation I craved, off I went to my father's. If it was clean sheets, full course meals, and spending money, hi, mom!

Mom's was the real home, and dad's, if you will, the tree house. If mom's was all about behaviour, dad's was a relief from it, the place where ideas, jokes, and attitudes would not be sanitized. A behavioural frontier land, spare, with eclectic, bare bones furniture reflecting the pervading dictums of freedom and rebellion.

Any imposition of the real world, any visitor from that other, stuffier planet, would suffer the same verbal buckshot by which Jason Robards, as the pre-hippie in *Clowns,* would eschew strangers from his colourful cocoon.

In a rare case of art imitating life, we even suffered the visits of a dotty female social worker, whose insistence that my father get over his mid-life crisis for the sake of his poor, suffering charge was rebuffed in the same sweet'n'sour style as Robards.

It was more fun watching them go at it than it was my mother and her husband, whose emotional to and fro had a lot less panache. When that couple's big final scene came, their parting, it was no Mary Tyler Moore versus Donald Sutherland. The fireworks were but ladyfingers. Still, the same message as in *Ordinary People* was thereby revealed: that in a world of creature comforts, the creature always triumphs over the comforts.

Within a few short years, there came a dramatic turning of the tables: dad became the respectable member of society (shades of *Clowns'* melancholy ending), mom the broke, introspective struggler.

There was no shuttling between two worlds for me by then, though. I had turned eighteen and was eager to set out into the larger world of which theirs had been idiosyncratic precursors.

And so I ventured, ready to leave the unique footprints fashioned by my formative years: one from a Salvation Army boot, the other from a careerist's dress shoe.

☆☆☆☆☆

HE BEGGED, he pleaded, he improvised deals.

Nothing, however, could make them bend the rules, those implacable guardians of the Elgin Theatre, stone-tempered arbiters of who got to see what. I was thirteen now and living with my father. Ontario, it ended up, had much stricter censorship rules than Quebec. An F word in a script, a tryst between co-stars, a lowbrow joke—each was enough to keep one such as I from its movie houses. It was a dire dictate no scheme of dad's, desperate for me to see his much-loved *One Flew Over the Cuckoo's Nest*, was going to upset.

As my father hung up on the theatre manager and explained to me that he had tried his best, I'm not sure which one of us had the longer face. He stewed a bit...then came up with a one more idea: he would pay for me to see the movie in the adjacent theatre while he paid for *Cuckoo's Nest*—then, somehow, he'd attempt to sneak me in. "No promises on that one though, son," he added in a voice all too aware of the risk. No promises was right; I knew those ushers at The Elgin. They were the toughest in the city. I could recite a list of the movies they had caught me attempting to sneak into that would last until my fourteenth birthday.

The next day, I received the consolation prize: the book, which my father had picked up while purchasing his daily pack of cigarettes. I tried to read it, but this wasn't the story I wanted. It was written from the Chief's point of view, a character my dad had told me didn't even speak! Having him recite the story instead of McMurphy was like giving Groucho's lines to Harpo.

Finally, almost an entire year later, the film moved from the prestigious Elgin to the faux hip Capitol Square. Now that was a theatre you could sneak into, what with those horny young ushers always busy sweet-talking the Breck Shampoo types who made popcorn.

I paid for a Charles Bronson film I had no intention of seeing, and when the solitary usher turned his back on me to try out a bad line on the giggling brunette behind the candy counter, ducked into a room illuminated only by the oversized faces of Jack Nicholson and Louise Fletcher.

I left just before the closing credits, through an unmanned side exit. As I emerged into the sunshine, I felt everything my father had told me I would feel: exhilarated, unnerved, riled...and yet, none of it had anything to do with the film.

Unlike McMurphy, I had bucked the system and won.

✰✰✰✰✰

EARTHQUAKES. Tidal waves. All-consuming fires.

We withstood them all, valiantly flirting with death, bravely rescuing whoever was losing that same gamble.

Torrents took apart walls, sending a life-threatening water-brick mix after us. Foot-high flames pursued us up every floor of the highest of high rises, until only the roof brought relief. Chunks of street were torn in half, as easily as sheets of foolscap, and only a few hurried steps prevented us from plunging into the crudely created chasm.

The small confine that was the perpetual prey of each of these debacles, week after week after week, should have been declared a disaster area.

Instead, like us, it emerged from it all more or less pristine, the only consequence a rumpled bed sheet or a fallen pillow.

It was a private world created by my giddy cousins and me, fuelled by homemade banana splits (thank you, *Memère*) and the proliferation of disaster pictures then occupying theatres.

With wide eyes and leaping hearts, we took in *The Poseidon Adventure*, *Earthquake*, and *The Towering Inferno*, and, in lulls between major releases, poor Japanese cousins like *Tidal Wave* or *Airport* rip-offs like *Skyjacked*.

They were the precursors of today's special-effects extravaganzas, the last action-packed events before the advent of CGI. They were also metaphors for a deteriorating world, one being torn apart, tornado-style, by morasses such as Vietnam and Watergate.

We, kids all, knew none of this—only the woozy, what's-going-to-happen-next thrill that came with confrontations between Charlton Heston and a falling lamppost or Paul Newman and an uncooperative fire door.

Minutes Away we called our amalgam of these films, the one we enacted and embellished every time we gathered in our much-loved *Memère's* smallish bedroom, hitherto an ad hoc Catholic shrine.

What Jesus, who looked down upon us from his picture-frame atop *Memère*`s bureau—which shook with every rapidly stomped foot and trembled with every fallen body—thought about all this, I can't imagine. Perhaps, in his own, quiet way, he was contentedly reveling in the sight of children at play—and not looking on indifferently, as he seemed to be doing over the adult world.

✯✯✯✯✯

WE WERE fellow travelers he and I, him with his straw-blonde hair and toothpaste-white smile, me, some years younger, with a stringy, unkempt, greasy mop and bottom teeth the victims of parental penury. Still, we had more in common than you might think—specifically, a boyish enthusiasm fuelled by the high of adventure and freedom.

I was thirteen, just thirteen, and, as an afterthought of a gift I guess, my father had just given me permission to go the movies by myself. By myself! An exhilarating first!

I was completely aware, with every step to the nearby bus stop, with every rickety mile the bus took, and with the secure feel of the warm summer air that continued to caress me as I ventured under the Somerset's two-sided marquee into its plush red lobby reeking of popcorn, that he—that dashing figure upon the screen just out of my sight—was experiencing the exact same thrill that I was.

The sky, in the era in which the film took place, was uncharted territory; the world of the movies, for me, the same. I had seen but a few, and wondered, much like flying ace Waldo Pepper, what lay beyond the known, what adventures, what disappointments.

Some two hours later, Waldo's journey ended, and so, as a result, did mine. To the simplistic, tinkly theme that has remained in my head to this day—though I have not seen the film in many a year—I exited into a fresh-feeling July evening, with the sounds of downtown Ottawa—the grumbles of drunkards, the cry of sirens, the hot roar of crisscrossing busses—intermingling under a pink and purple sky. Though I had left the confines of the Somerset, I was awestruck once again; never before had I experienced this, the added bonus of another kind of poetry, the urban landscape at nightfall.

As I stood there, drinking it all in, I realized that though I was no longer flying alongside Waldo, I was flying still; that the tradition of what the two of us had shared was living on.

✯✯✯✯✯

THE MOVIE we were there to see, my younger sister and I, was in the adjacent theatre. It was yet another Disney flick: *That Darn Cat*, starring the studio's squeaky stalwart, Dean Jones. At thirteen, the forced innocence of these things was beginning to wear thin. About halfway through, I mumbled something about the men's room and excused myself.

Stepping out into the red velour lobby, it occurred to me that the usher, the skinny, mop-topped boy with the aviator glasses and the off-yellow wide legs, had disappeared. This, I realized, was it. My chance.

American Graffiti was a film I had heard a lot about—nothing specific, just rumblings from stuffy parents about its shockingly generous rating. Any fourteen-year-old could fork over his paper route savings and be corrupted by images of fast cars, sexual escapades, and other forms of post-war debauchery. Thinking back on it now, what they probably resented was the misrepresentation of their era, their strictly enforced Eisenhower haircuts and conservative flirting reconceived as a So Cal Sodom and Gomorrah.

Whatever the cause, their rumblings had sold me harder than any fast-paced television preview. I slid into a tiny, opportune crack between that theatre's doors, and entered a veritable wonderland. Before me, big as life, danced the swirling colours, swift pace, and relentless, energic music of the Lucas-created Fifties.

This was not a movie I was watching. This was a long, hypnotic stare into a crystal ball.

I had no idea, up until that moment, that movies could hold another purpose, that they were not just entertainments but living landscapes of imitable behaviours played out by outsized role models.

There was Toad, the four-eyed, funny-in-spite-of-himself runt of the ensemble. He was undersized, myopic, and as awkward as I was promising to be. I could see myself, tragically, growing into him. There I am, four, five years from now, I began to fear, ramming my scooter into a vending machine!

What I aspired to, as the film rolled on, was Curt—not classically handsome, not inordinately charming, but likeable, slightly neurotic, and the possessor of a semi-secret talent for big-picture observation.

A tug at my pants. Shit! The usher! No. My sister.

I walked her back to the company of Dean Jones, just as *Graffiti* was coming to its end. Terry the Toad, the screen began to read, rewarding its audience with a post-story rundown of the lives they had been watching, went missing in action in Vietnam. "Curt Henderson is a writer," it continued, "living in Canada."

Ah ha!, I told myself. So, I can be Curt.

ACT TWO

"I SAW *Jaws* again the other night."

To the others, this was an abrupt but meaningless confession. For my cousins and I, about a third of the gathering, this announcement was a ticket to a time machine.

Instantly, we were transported from a suburban Christmas dinner table to a downtown sidewalk in the blazing heat, then, converted from a trio of parents playing middle-aged catch-up to a gaggle of giddy pre-teens unable to civilize themselves.

There we all were, outside the sizeable Nelson, back when movies for the under-fourteen set cost a dollar, a sum even we found easy to come by—so easy, in fact, that attending screenings of *Jaws* became our defining summer ritual. Grander, parent-engineered events, like vacations to faraway lands, in-town trips of cultural interest, even the much-anticipated excursion to the annual fair, became giant distractions, sneaky schemes to unfairly wrench us from the playground we never wanted to leave, the dark, anticipatory confines of the Nelson, as it pulsed to John Williams' minimalist basso.

How many times did we see it?

Once a day I seem to remember, but it was probably more like once a week, maybe once every two weeks.

If that number strikes me as low, it's because all of the time in between was spent animatedly recounting our favourite moments, or clipping images of the film from newspapers and magazines, or talking it up to our parents (each of whom thought we were nuts, naturally) or, like many a group of kids that summer, acting the film out in public pools; you couldn't find a facility in North America that season without at least one child cast as a shark and all of his or her companions as prospective snacks.

A voice (an uncle? An aunt?) hemmed or coughed or started up about something in the news, and the deep and unspoken link between my cousins and I was broken. The summer sun set and again it was Christmas, thirty-five years on.

As exchanges of various qualities made their way around the room like cranberry sauce, I began to examine the cousin who had uttered the opening line, prompting the secret visual handshake of the sacred *Jaws* brotherhood. She was as vivacious as ever, if worn at the edges, suffering the early burdens of single motherhood. The other member of the brethren, her equally bubbly but bothered sister, was now contributing something about recent business problems, while I, internally, was toying with laying my recent career crisis on the table like a steaming bowl of mashed potatoes.

We were face to face now, Robert Shaw style, with the shark; soon, blood would either be pouring out of our mouths or we would be swimming safely toward a new horizon.

✩✩✩✩✩

THE PAPERS WERE DELIVERED around four o'clock, about the time I got home from school. I would take the elevator up to our floor. The door would open, and there they'd be, lined up before each apartment like paper welcome mats—each apartment, that is, but ours.

I would look around—an empty ritual but who knew? There might always be that odd day where somebody would come home from work early, not the usual five thirty or six o'clock—and help myself to one—a different one each day, of course; I couldn't risk suspicion by going serial.

I would then hide it among my homework, walk into our apartment, and greet my father.

After closing my bedroom door on some convincing premise about the requirement of absolute concentration, I would carefully lay the paper out, close enough to the edge of the bed so that, at the sudden sound of anybody entering, I could quickly slip the contraband beneath it. Slowly, I pored over each page, drinking in the faces and names of my favourite stars, and/or the artwork of each piece of promotional propaganda.

After selecting my prized pieces, I would proceed, with my trustily silent school scissors, to cut out whatever it was I had deemed the day's keepsakes, leaving great big square holes in an otherwise pristine evening edition.

I would then silently open my bottom drawer and add the new images to those hidden under tidy piles of underwear and socks, where they would lay until taken out again to be treasured anew in the next stolen moment.

After finishing my homework, I would complete my criminality by stuffing the paper carefully inside my clothing, making some excuse to leave the apartment, such as volunteering to get that one ingredient that would make that night's dinner extra special.

Setting out, I would silently return the paper, sans select images, to the apartment from which it had been plucked, then be on my merry way to the smallish strip mall across the street, thrilled that I had lived—in other words, not been caught—to snip another day.

At night, while attempting to sleep, I would sometimes hear rumblings through the apartment-thin walls. I often wondered if they were Charlie or Harry, the kind of old fashioned, middle-aged grump I imagined inhabited the other apartments on our floor, finally getting to the evening's paper, and bitching at Mildred or Harriet, through a mysterious rectangle, about what the hell might be going on at The Ottawa Citizen.

✪✪✪✪✪

Its battered carcass had been dragged through the deepest reaches of the Amazon, its teakettle hide painted by sun and swamp. It had run afoul of animals and armies, and had endured insufferable passengers, including a missionary's difficult sister, who broke its hull of a heart, ultimately, by helping herself to the only thing that ever loved it: a smalltime opportunist with a seven-day growth and a history of hangovers.

I am speaking of the venerable riverboat from John Huston's *The African Queen,* which, a half century ago or more, sailed African bush and Hollywood back lot, bringing Katherine Hepburn to Humphrey Bogart and a loose wing of the Nazi party to an ironic end.

None of the indignities it suffered onscreen, however, could match the sheer misery it was enduring now: there she was—I had seen its picture in the papers, had snipped it out probably—claustrophobically trapped in a truck, separated from the rest of civilization by a panel of rusting mesh.

Its lonely appearance reminded one not of Huston, Katie, and Bogie but of Walt Disney: the famous scene from *Dumbo,* where the pining pachyderm protagonist sits separated from its mother.

Then again, what was there to be separated from? The torrential rain on this particular night, a Tuesday at that, when no one went out, was surely keeping even the most die-hard movie lover away. Hell, it was even keeping *me* away!

No amount of prayer recited at the windows of my mother's home—a good series of bus rides away from where this poor, metallic animal, which deserved a far better version of its one-night stay in our city, was sitting—would bring relief. I was becoming certain, if that boat could speak, that it would confess that for all of its globetrotting time with Huston and company, it had never experienced anything like this.

I was not going to see it then—not until tomorrow, I knew, would this blasted rain finally let up, leaving a large, uninteresting puddle in place of this rare link to Hollywood's golden age, there at the foot of Bogie's Lounge, the enterprising bar in Vanier, the lowest-rent area of the city, which had somehow managed to wrangle this fly-by-night exhibit to honour its namesake.

The door to our home opened. My mother, late from work and soaking wet (despite her umbrella), entered. "I saw it, son. I stood in front of it for fifteen minutes."

I knew immediately what she was talking about, for we had discussed the movie—a mutual favourite—and my penchant for seeing one of its artifacts the day before. "I hope you're happy," she added, shaking light bulb-sized drops from limp strands of her usually hairspray-hard hair. "I did it for you, son. Only for you."

My Queen.

✩✩✩✩✩

SPIDERMAN. Superman. Batman.

One night, from the balcony of the ground floor apartment I shared with my father, I heard them.

One was attempting to stop an oncoming submarine when another, swimming toward the sub himself, broke through the waves to argue with him. "Superman can't swim!" he challenged, claiming the potential glory of stopping the sub for himself. "Yes, he can!" countered Superman. "He's Superman!"

Had these eight-year-olds had a Saturday morning cartoon to watch, a big budget superhero movie they could attend (a genre in short supply back then, before Hollywood's Marvel mania) or even reruns of the Adam West series to enjoy, they would know exactly what the respective superheroes they chose to impersonate could and could not do. But this was the age of low visibility for such types, so alas, the fight raged on.

"Okay, okay!" it was frustratingly decided, "Let's start over. I'll be Batman!" "And I'll be Robin!" added the other, choosing a persona decidedly less powerful than that of his friend's in order to avoid more skirmishes.

Batman and Robin...hmm...this gave me an idea!

While the dynamic duo, in their makeshift beach-towel-and-clothes-pin capes, began to brainstorm who they would battle and why, I, much older, was deciding what they needed was an awe-inspiring call to action.

I dug up a bulky old portable light that was part of my father's photographic equipment. I then found a piece of construction paper and began to cut out the stylish image of a bat. Affixing it to the light with scotch tape, I thus created what would be, once I turned it on, a perfect replica of the famous hero-conjuring bat signal.

The kids, I knew, had not grown up with the aforementioned series, but if I pointed out its sudden appearance in the sky above their heads and explained its significance, I was sure they would both feel that the quality of their play had been serendipitously enhanced, and be mighty impressed with their voyeuristic and enterprising neighbour two balconies over.

I pointed my first-ever, self-made special effect toward the sky, stole a glance of my soon to be awed audience, and turned on the light...a light so powerful that the paper went up in a ball of raging fire, leaving me stomping and screaming like a madman, wrestling with the flame that was threatening to make its way into the house and burn down the apartment.

Instead of a mock version of Commissioner Gordon flashing the bat signal, what Batman and Robin caught was a screaming, panicking pre-teen with smoke pouring out of the ends of his bell bottoms.

The worst part: they didn't even come to my rescue.

✰✰✰✰✰

SHE WAS the first alliteration I had ever met.

Often, in fact, I wondered if the attraction my male classmates felt for her wasn't entirely attributable to the sound of her name—for, to be frank, while attractive in a fresh-faced kind of way, she would have held up little in an arena offering genuine variety.

This was, after all, a small school—grades seven to ten—exclusively populated by the working- class Irish, Italian and French who lived in the surrounding area. Its squatty, autumn-bricked confines smelled constantly of the stomach-churning combination of sweat, steamed hot dogs, and pencil shavings. And while the teachers were sufficiently extending, but a few, with the exception of a pipe-smoking, older-than-his-looks history teacher, suggested candidacy for a more legitimate place of learning.

One fateful morning, I took an enormous chance. In this atmosphere of miniature macho men and strategically protective girls, I brought a movie magazine—the only kind there was in those days, the kind mothers read while sitting in beauty parlors, their heads fitted to dryers resembling oversized Mix Masters. It was Barbra Streisand, I recall, who graced its cover.

The magazine's only true attraction to me (did people really care about all of that idle gossip?) was the colour insert that served as its heart: a half-dozen images from the latest box office hit, splashily laid out.

The intention was to find, semi-subversively, a fellow movie fan. It was an odd way to do it but burgeoning, irrepressible movie-lover that I was, I was desperate. And while I didn't pine for her the way that others did, a part of me hoped, for mostly ego-boosting reasons, that it *would* be her, the gilded alliteration.

And impress her, to my surprise, I did. Within seconds of

spotting Barbra's iconic nose, she was all over me. In time, the other members of her privileged entourage joined us, and for a quick, unexpected moment, I found myself the envy and ire of each of my male classmates. It lasted until the circle tightened around me, and the magazine disappeared in the throng. Then, the girls disappeared too, the alliteration leading them God knew where for a closer examination of the magazine.

End of day. The alliteration approaches me, at my locker, one more time—for the last time, in fact, in my life. She smiles (I briefly see, in the way it alters her defensiveness, what the more intuitive might have noted in her) and presents me with what remains of the magazine: but Barbra's nose. Her smile turns into a laugh and I into the streets.

Still, I leave with what I came for—an alliteration: fuck finding a fellow film fan!

☆☆☆☆☆

"I REMEMBER when this was the Nelson," I volunteered, as my wife and I, take-out lattes in hand, strolled past the Bytowne, Ottawa's premiere art house, with its line-up of twenty-somethings eager to catch some obscure documentary from South Africa or Indonesia.

"That pizza place across the street, that was a Harvey's," I continued. My wife, accustomed to this newfound nostalgia of mine (middle-age), indulges me with a hollow smile.

"In 1976, the Nelson was playing a revival of *2001: A Space Odyssey*. Me and some guys from junior high school went to see it. We hung out afterwards in the Harvey's because at fourteen, their hot dogs were all we could afford."

They were sci-fi lovers, my set, all of them. Their chatter was populated by buzzwords like Asimov, Bradbury, Lovecraft, and Clark.

I could never hide the fact that I was the square peg that

didn't fit their black hole, that my love was for something else, something they deemed intellectually lesser: the movies.

Usually, it was me, slowly circling—much like the arty ships in the movie—their vast, mysterious universe, with its unfathomable secrets, its cryptic intelligence, its hermetic boastfulness.

On Remembrance Day, we would play hooky and go to Parliament Hill. They would make a game of naming each honoured regiment...during leisure hours, they would play chess, conduct science experiments, have day-long Risk tournaments...in the schoolyard, where we would exchange witticisms, they would spout bon mots worthy of Mad Magazine or even, on a good day, Monty Python.

And yet, each step of the way...they included me.

Did I make them feel superior? Were they trying to mentor me? Was I just another one of their intellectual challenges?

Or, in some way of which I was not entirely conscious, did I actually...fit in?

"We had this huge debate about whether or not those were real apes in the opening sequence or if they were men in suits."

"And?" my still willing wife indulged. "What did you decide?"

"That they were probably both," I answered, as we neared our car and our rare excursion into the city's core concluded. "A gorilla's a gorilla."

✯✯✯✯✯

EACH CATCHPHRASE, each sight gag, each throwaway was met by the same thing: synchronized giggles accompanied by a chorus of clicks.

So persuasive did that aural union become that, after awhile, heads, most white, blue or bald, began to turn.

The laughter they could tolerate, even if it was the unrestricted, adolescent variety, not the stifled, polite type they were letting out, in spite of their better natures.

But the clicking, that remained, to them, a mystery, an unreasonable upset of ritual, like a hole burned in the film or a reel unprofessionally out of place. What could its source possibly be, they wondered, squinting at our dark, slumped forms.

And just what are these annoying teens doing here on a weekday afternoon, huddled with we retirees? Shouldn't they be in school? Then again, they considered, perhaps it's the continual clicking of someone's dentures, prying loose whenever those high-pitched knights in the bullet-shaped hats squeak "Ni!" or whenever those naughty bits of arcane animation disrupt-enhance the narrative.

They would never know, for we, much more able bodied than they, would spring out of downtown's Capitol Square Theatre faster than they could, the first to integrate the high of this experience, the much-anticipated *Monty Python and the Holy Grail*, with the other blessings of the day: the early summer sunshine, the first afternoon of the last day of middle school, the last precious stage of our brotherly bond, the latter soon to be severed, bit by bit, by girls, jobs, and societal surprises of which we weren't yet aware.

Down the streets we walked, laughing, remembering, quoting, annoying all and sundry whom we passed—including, after a stop for an especially raucous lunch, those seniors—again!—the same sensitive ones who had suffered through the experience of our attendance at the theatre.

It seemed miles, years, millennia between us—the young, vigorous, and loud contrasted with the aged, stern and quiet.

"Hey!" we all shouted, "Check it out." So saying, we all brandished the rusted metal objects fastened securely to the front of our belt loops: our locks, which, upon being freed from academic indenture that morning, we had each taken off of our locker and secured to our person before taking in the celebratory matinee.

Mystery solved, as each of us again fiddled with the tumblers for the sake of the seniors.

Finally, a smile came out of them, followed by a laugh much bigger than any they had released within the confines of the theatre.

We, their diminutive disciples, had bested Monty Python.

The locks were indeed off, and the world was ours.

✯✯✯✯✯

A DOZEN PAIRS of eyes were upon me, each with that same cynical expression.

They remained fixed as I shuffled humbly about the room, doing my best to look emotionally crippled and imminently curable.

They continued to look on as a dialogue developed between myself and the gray-haired man in the non-descript suit, just off the noisy concession stand from which the smell of melted butter wafted.

"I'm sorry," he explained in a tone kind but firm. "Those have to go back to the distributor."

The "distributor"—whatever that was. I tried again, a little less quietly this time, exchanging the search for sympathy for my all-consuming passion for the movies.

When I got a small smile out of him, I thought perhaps that I had reached it: the turning point. What would surely follow would be a, "Welllll…if it means that much to you, son…"

It was not to be. He stood fast to his professional obligations, and no movie-crazy pre-teen was going to change his mind, no matter how desperate or obsessed that greasy-haired young man appeared to be.

The expressions of the members of the comic army that he

kept behind him—in their regulation uniforms of suit, cigar and walking stick—remained unchanged…and yet, their sneers seemed to have intensified. I would not be taking them home after all, these photos of W.C. Fields, which just last week had begun to grace the theatre in conjunction with the new biopic of his life.

They would remain where they were, Fields' face reveling in the pain of my failure (happy, toddler-hating fusspot that he was), in the fact that a child of need had just had an adult snub him so decidedly.

I considered trying again, but by the time my eyes fell from the silent sneer of the endless Fields' to the off-white head of the manager, he was bidding me a curt goodbye.

I left, realizing that no matter what argument I presented, I had no right to those photographs—not because they had to go back to some "distributor," but because it was he who belonged in Fields' company, not I.

✯✯✯✯✯

IT WAS BLACK, had buttons the size of chocolate chip cookies, and went down past my knees. It weighed more than I did, and as a result, no doubt contributed to my already slouchy appearance.

Its best feature, though, was hidden to the eye.

If you slipped your hand into the left pocket, your fingers would continue past the torn lining. If your arms were long enough—and no one's, excepting the then popular Harlem Globetrotters' maybe, were—you might be able to touch the very hem of this extremely long coat. And if you were dexterous enough—and again, nobody was—you might be able to bring your hand from that particular area all the way round to the bottom of the coat's middle, a deep, dark no man's land not even a speck of lint had ever found its way to.

Whether or not this coat had this accidental feature when I first inherited it, I don't remember—only that its existence seriously furthered, by way of fattening my book collection, my love of movies.

For if, say, you were a poor, movie-struck kid with a touch of the juvenile delinquent about you, you could sneak a thin, glossy novelization of the latest cinematic hit into that serendipitous receptacle, where it would silently drop to the bottom. Then, by fastening your coat a little too jerkily, you could nonchalantly work the book all the way to that special spot at the rear, where no store detective, should he have framed you in his eagle eye, could find it, even if he put his hand through the hole.

Don't get me wrong. I did not like the idea of stealing things. It was simply the easiest way I knew to get my fix, to enjoy, in some semblance, the movies I could not afford to go to, or that were restricted to me by virtue of the censorship of the times.

It was also, I thrillingly discovered, a great way to meet intelligent and sexually curious girls.

It started when I spotted one on a bus, reading the new edition of *Looking for Mr. Goodbar*, the one that tied-in to the then just released movie version, and going over the choicest passages.

Inspired, I swiped a copy, read it, and had basis for conversation with a class of female hitherto completely out of my league. In time, this became a ritual repeated over many a controversial female-themed movie.

Winters came and went. I eschewed my wanton ways, I tried my hand at menial jobs, I earned money.

I outgrew the coat, too...or maybe I just ditched it. I hope not ungratefully.

Every now and then, however, the grown-up me finds himself light on spending cash, and sees an intriguing young woman reading a risqué movie adaptation on a bus.

I curse my Old Navy-purchased pea coat and those bastards behind bar codes.

☆☆☆☆☆

"BEWARE THE IDES OF MARX."

It was a bad pun but worthy of Groucho nevertheless. Why then, did it irritate him so, every time Josef von Sternberg, the stylish melodramatist responsible for the career of Marlene Dietrich, cracked it? Perhaps ol' Grouch had been simply miffed that he didn't think of it first. It was a line I would have appreciated, though, had try-too-hard Joe directed it at me—advice, in fact, I sorely could have used.

The national longing for all things Thirties, born out of the three-tragedy-pile-up of Oswald, Vietnam, and Watergate, had yet to die. Revival houses continued to proliferate, like clichés in a Barbara Stanwyck movie. Ours, for better or worse, was the Towne Cinema, the fire hazard with a colonial name, on the edge of one of the roughest neighbourhoods in the city (since, of course, gentrified).

I sat discreetly at the back, away from anyone potentially dangerous—anyone taller, older or bigger. The first film, *At the Circus*, rolled. We all, a hundred or so of us, laughed—all of us, that is, but him: the lanky, half-seen presence a row or two ahead of me, enveloped in a curious cloud of blue-gray smoke. Groucho leered, Harpo mugged, Chico played, Mr. Mysterio smoked...smoked, in fact, until his once hearty ability to laugh audibly deteriorated into a hermetic silence. Was this what marijuana (for by now, I had figured out what it was) did to you? This indulgence I had vowed, no matter how much the 'stoners' at my school made fun of me, never to sample?

Little did I know that this would be the day this vow, despite my best efforts, was destined to be broken. Halfway through *The Big Store*, I too, like the subversive corruptor of model youth slumped strategically ahead of me, had started to find the punch lines progressively less funny. Oh no, I thought, it's getting to me! I tried holding my breath, my nose...my breath and my nose. Finally, when *Love Happy* failed to illicit a single chortle from me, I left, convinced that I was now no better than the lowest element in the school yard.

It wasn't until *Duck Soup*, a few weeks later on television, that I stopped experiencing a guilt-ridden sense of kinship every time I passed those kids in the hall with the red eyes and the bad report cards. I had simply been a victim, I finally figured out, of tired, late era Marxiana, not of primo, contraband Mexicana.

Beware the ides of Marx indeed.

✯✯✯✯✯

BACK IN THAT ERA—THE late Seventies—they were just starting to pop up in Canada's major cities: Toronto. Montreal, Vancouver, hot on the heels of a new tax incentive and a drooping dollar that was luring Hollywood, slowly but surely, to a colder clime.

They were mostly B list names but heck, I didn't care. A star —any star—would do, regardless of how far he or she had fallen from the filmic firmament.

Toronto, though, could have been just as remote as L.A., and Montreal, though only half the distance away, the same; neither of my parents ever left Ottawa to re-visit it.

The space between my nose and the newspaper then, the star *du jour*'s face staring back at me from the Toronto-based photo therein, would be the ultimate proximity between myself and any cinematic icon—at least, I dreamed, until that fateful day when I would head for Hollywood myself.

You can estimate how high my heart leaped, then, when I discovered that none other than Danny Kaye, a boyhood idol, would be making a one day stop in the country's capital a.k.a. my backyard.

Ottawa may not have had any moviemaking infrastructure, but what it did have was the seat of government. As such, it was a prime stage for celebrities stumping political causes.

Kaye had just been crowned the ambassador for UNICEF (he'd be followed by Peter Ustinov, Audrey Hepburn, and Roger Moore) and it was in that capacity that he would be putting in an hour or two with our then Prime Minister, the movie star-esque Pierre Trudeau.

Unbeknownst to my mother, with whom I was living half the time, I skipped school that afternoon and spent my time in the lobby of the House of Commons. There, I grilled puzzled gatekeepers and uninterested reporters until I was asked, with classic Canadian politesse, to leave.

After a half hour or so outside, I was obliged to go home, lest I give away where I had actually been.

The next day, my heart broke as photos of Kaye appeared all over the newspaper. Where in the building had he been? What time had he been here? What entrance and/or exit had he used?

That Halloween, my first as greeter, endless kids presented me with boxes for UNICEF.

I saved my pennies for Hollywood.

☆☆☆☆☆

HAD he ever played a smaller house?

Back in the days of vaudeville perhaps, when, according to the other comics, he didn't yet have an act. But certainly not since making a name for himself, starting with his regular radio appearances in the Thirties.

This, then, was his most sparse audience in ages—just myself and a half-dozen others. Then again, nobody was expected at all; this was, after all, simply a sound check.

Still, I (and I guess the few others) just had to be here, had to get as much of him as we could while he was, improbably, around. Comic names his size rarely graced our city with their holy presences.

Thank God for the Ex, what everyone in the city called the annual summer fair. Hitherto, I had hated it—all those fast rides that made you throw up all that greasy, overpriced food. But every now and again, they brought in an act that redeemed, at least in my eyes, the entire affair.

Bob continued, and we giggled appreciatively over each one-liner—maybe even loud enough that he could hear us—relishing every familiar "But I gotta tell ya..." that got him from joke to joke to joke.

I watched, remembering the book that I had in the pocket of my warm-up jacket, the one I had brought to pass the time while I waited for the slope-nosed Messiah, and wondered which of the names therein would aspire to his mantle. It seemed unlikely that any of them would, their shaggy hair and adult material a stark contrast to his gentlemanly countenance and family-friendly wit. Somehow, though, I knew that times would change, and that either Gabe Kaplan or Robert Klein or Jay Leno would become the new Bob Hope.

The mikes met with Bob's approval, and soon, the few of us who were there doubled, tripled, quadrupled. The band struck up his theme song, and Bob, leading the way with a golf club, strode upon the stage.

Though I had heard all of the material, I still laughed. It was not unlike my book, the one with the transcriptions of all the contemporary comics' routines. No matter how many times I read them, they still made me chortle appreciatively.

The show ended with a standing ovation (of course!) and I left high on the thrill that I had spent time in the company of a living legend.

The bus home hit an especially long red light. I reached into my pocket, looking for......my book! My book with all those comedy routines in it! It was gone!

Worse, it had my one souvenir of Bob in it: my ticket stub from the show!

Was it too late to hop off the bus to go and look for it? Damn! By now, the fairgrounds would be closed!

The next day, still in a state of inconsolable despair, I ventured from the apartment I shared with my father to our corner store to get him some cigarettes (yes, they sold them to minors back then). Walking by the used paperback display, I noticed something; another copy of it, that book, that book that I so coveted!

I grabbed it. Its front pages held another surprise: there it was, tucked undisturbed between monologues by Joan Rivers and Richard Pryor: my souvenir of Bob!

This was my book, mine, the one! Some enterprising so and so had obviously come across it after I had left it behind and had sold it for some chump change! He hadn't even bothered to rifle through its pages; he didn't even know what a treasure he had held! Ha!!!

The cashier busy with a fussy customer, I sneakily slipped the book back into the wooly pocket that was its estranged home.

One pack of cigarettes later, myself, accompanied by some of the hottest rising comics in the industry—and better still, proof positive of my audience with Bob Hope—left the store.

Hey, storekeep: thanks for the memories!

✯✯✯✯✯

MY BIGGEST FEAR was that I'd spoil it for him.

Deprive him, my best friend, of what I had undergone not days ago: the cinematic validation of our working-class lives. Not only were nobodies like us worthy of movie-screen sized attention, it affirmed, we might very well be the stuff of urban fairy tales.

I couldn't do it. And yet, I owed him. Big time. After all, he had adopted me...me, anonymous me—strategically anonymous, in order to spare myself the undue attention of school bullies—by him, the coolest guy in school, the guy at ease with both the tough guys and the frail. Why he selected me I still don't know; the instinct to protect, I guess—as much a part of him as of the title character in the newly opened film I was about to describe to him, *Rocky*.

What had gotten me into this pickle? Girls. Two of them—neither of which I had ever met. He was seeing both. He had told the first, before a date with the second, that he was going to the movies with yours truly. Therefore, in order to cover his behind...

I started, slowly, like the film itself. Then, continuing to convey its rhythm, I kept building, building, building...

My description of the movie was a revelation to me. As he sat there on that worn couch in that under-lit apartment—in rooms very much like those in the movie, rooms the two of us had known all our lives—I described every scene not only in order, but in painstaking detail, with sample after sample of its dialogue. I had only seen it once but here I was, recounting it as if I, and not Sylvester Stallone, had conceived the entire thing.

I had no idea that movies could get under my skin like that; that I could absorb them the way the tape on Rocky's hands had absorbed cow's blood; that I could spit them back out again with the zeal and emphasis with which Rocky's trainer, Burgess Meredith's Mickey, had spat out words of hard-earned wisdom.

When I finished, I too, like Adrian's comforting embrace, received a reward: my friend's recitation of everything I had said.

Sometime later, he recounted the story of the movie, just as I had to him, to the girl, who totally bought, as a consequence, that he'd been out with me. How could she not?

A part of me, a big part, would have rather that he had incurred her wrath, that he had suffered her nails to his face rather than to miss out on the first-hand experience of this movie. To my movie-loving mind, his getting mauled as badly as Rocky, as much as I cared for him, would have been the smallest of prices.

A few days later, I received the phone call. "Danny!" he shouted, "I saw it! I saw it!" He didn't have to add more. I knew by his excited tone exactly what he was referring to—and that this movie was so good that nothing, not even the intense passion of a movie-lover let loose, could spoil it for anyone.

☆☆☆☆☆

"WHO WAS SHE," he asked, "the wife?"

Uh huh, I affirmed.

"She was good too," he conceded. Then, another overlong groan made its way through the wall—his cue to high-tail it from the smallish living room to the even smaller bedroom.

She had been at it all night, splitting the focus of my world between the Academy Awards and the inconceivable prospect that she might soon die—so inconceivable that the broadcast took on an even greater significance than usual for me. It became a portal through which I could escape, something I could stay focused on to distract me from the ugly reality lurking just beyond the wall.

There was some murmuring from her dutiful son, my uncle, another award for *Network*, then more murmuring. A commercial for the GMC Pacer, then, finally, silence, permitting my uncle to re-enter the room, just as the Awards were ramping up again.

"It's a great movie," he said, endorsing what was looking like a sweep for *Network*. "It's a shame that they won't let you see it." Due to a gabby Faye Dunaway atop a lucky William Holden, the film was off limits to we fifteen-year-olds. "The message it has about the today's generation and television..."

Another groan. Off he went again.

A tacky musical number, a staple of the Awards in those days, began—so bad and so uninteresting that try as I might, I could not keep my mind off the now even more audible pain that my much-loved *Memère* was in.

I had become her charge in those years, not wanting to semi-live with my mother anymore and no longer able to live with my father, as he was now between jobs. It was just we two in that undersized apartment, with only whoever appeared on TV—in tonight's case, the world's biggest stars—as occasional company.

Tonight, though, after the stomach pains and the groaning had started, another guest had arrived: my uncle—where was my father?—whom I had been urged to call just before the Oscars, when all the trouble started.

By evening's end, a surprise knockout by *Rocky*, the exclamations of pain from my grandmother had ceased, replaced by a merciful snoring. My uncle was gone. I was left to turn off the television and to put myself to bed.

She was going to live, and tomorrow, though I would be sleepy, would be just another day.

How had I gotten through this ridiculous and trying evening?

"Today's generation and television..."

✩✩✩✩✩

I KNEW from the beginning that it wasn't going to last.

Despite my most desperate of hopes, there was no way that a

city this size, I realized even at that tender age, held enough movie lovers to keep such an enterprise alive.

They knew it, too—the evidence was the rock records and the counter-culture posters that, over the weeks that I had begun frequenting the place, were growing more and more abundant.

Nevertheless, each time someone, usually in shaggy hair and buckskin jacket, reeking of odors still largely foreign to me, came in and purchased a Led Zeppelin or a Jethro Tull, I felt an enormous relief inside my body, like a wobbly elevator ride coming to a smooth stop. It meant that the shop, this hidden jewel, this answer to my every movie lover's prayer, would remain open a little while longer—long enough, I hoped, for me to keep shoplifting its treasures.

Some were worn, some suffered from splotches of white-out or still sticky remnants of sacrilegiously affixed labels; nevertheless, there they were, stills upon stills upon stills, lined one behind the other like index cards in library drawers. Anything you wanted, any keepsake from any film, was at your imminent disposal: Lawrence upon his camel...Alvy kissing Annie... Clouseau performing an accidental trick dive.

I can't recall what they were asking for them; I'm sure it was well below what they'd be worth today, before the collector-mania that became one of the driving forces of the Baby Boomer economy of the Eighties. Whatever it was, it was too expensive for me, a kid who didn't even receive an allowance.

At least once a week, after school, I would sneak on to the wrong school bus and get to the shop, situated across from the city's only art house, the venerable Towne Cinema. I'd walk in as unobtrusively as possible, schoolbooks in arm, and begin to peruse the inventory. It was junk, I knew, to those that ran the theatre; promotional materials long past their robustness, on which they were looking to make a fast buck as an alternative to throwing them out. But one man's etc. as they say. And so, in just as quiet a manner as when I entered, I slyly began to slip select stills among my books and papers.

I told nothing of this to my school mates, despite the fact that I was desperate to brag not only of my finds but of my prowess as a thief. They'd think me an idiot regarding the former—stealing movie stills when I just as easily could have made away with a two LP Led Zeppelin?!—and might report the latter to a teacher, who then might tell it to my parents, who then might tell it to the shopkeep, who then might tell it to the cops.

Therefore, I said nothing—till the day that I proudly made off with oversized wedding photos of the Corleone family. I arrived at the secret lair that was my room to discover that in the bargain, I had also made away with—yes!—a two LP set of Led Zeppelin.

Interestingly, it was the first time that I had experienced something that hitherto, I had felt not even the slightest hint of: guilt.

The next day, after showing the record off to my friends and basking in their endless "Right On!"s, I boarded the wrong school bus again and reversed my earlier actions, slyly putting the disk back from where it came.

I walked out and never entered the shop again, as, predictably, it closed but a few months later.

Occasionally, I tally just how often, all these years later, that I think about the place. In the end, then, it was the store that stole from me.

✰✰✰✰✰

"I'M NOT GOING to any movie with a princess in it!"

So declared my sister, upon my suggestion that warm summer night that we—my mother, my stepfather, my sister, and I—head off to the nearest drive-in.

"That settles it!" added my stepfather, sternly. "We're not spending that kind of money if there's nothing anybody wants to see!"

And what was it, exactly, that they wanted to see? Action, laughs, and in my mother's case, a little romance. Thus, she became my sole ally in this battle to procure my all-consuming fix: the movies.

"Come on," she appealed to her ungiving husband in her best little girl's voice, "it will be fun."

And so, strictly to appease yours truly, and perhaps, a little, my mom, we all squeezed into the car and headed off.

The ride, while yes, a bit of a distance—the Auto-Sky Drive-In—felt like it took, thanks to the temperaments of those around me, what felt like hours. "I still don't know why in hell we're doing this!" my stepfather continued to bark. "This is going to be soooo stupid!" added my still unhappy sister. "Okay, okay, all of you"—mom, my staunch defender—"I've had enough!"

Finally, our tires hit the gravel indicating the drive-in. Small billows of dirty smoke began to emanate from our tires, until we pulled up before the screen. More bitching, more moaning, more complaining. "This better be worth it!" My stepfather again. My sister, now thankfully silent, had drifted off to a protesting sleep.

Minutes later, as the sky above turned from light blue to pink-yellow, the enormous screen before our car—and the dozen or so other cars in this largely unpopulated lot, as the film had just opened, came alive—*Alive!*—with a deep, quiet rumble and a long, slow view of a site hitherto unseen by moviegoers, reluctant or addicted, since cinema's inception: the underside of a navy carrier-sized spaceship. Soon, we were watching an imposing figure in shiny black plastic prepare to do battle with a naïve desert dweller who had become friends with a pair of Laurel and Hardy-like robots.

By the time the screen was busier than hell with pink and blue laser beams, sound effect upon sound effect, and plastic-faced creatures created by a crossbreed of Walt Disney and Hieronymus Bosch, even the anticipated appearance of the princess failed to return the family to its unhappy ways.

"How 'bout some popcorn?" I asked, cheekily testing my converts. "I'm not going!" answered my stepfather, riveted. "Don't look at me," answered my mother, taken by the romantic tension between the princess and the hero's best friend.

"No way!" contended my sister, still chuckling at the tinny banter between the robots, her words and tone the ultimate affirmation of my triumph. "I'm not missing any of this!"

I didn't venture from the car either, of course, as we all sat taking in every moment, perhaps the only bonding agent this new family had ever, would ever, know.

The battle, both Luke Skywalker's and mine, was finally won, with the destruction of the Death Star and the collective reaction of those around me, headed by my stepfather.

"Wow!" he pronounced, shaking his head in synch to the cacophony of the blasting car horns—a drive-in ritual of mass approval—as we filed out into the darkness. Turning to me, he added, "Great pick, kid!"

Despite what the screen had shown us, Luke and Darth were allies.

✩✩✩✩✩

"AND ARE THEY BULLETS?" asked the shorter one wearing the toque.

"They're laser beams," explained the one rubbing his bare hands to get them warm.

As he pointed to yet another lobby card crowding the window of the Somerset Theatre—marshmallow-looking robot men pointing newfangled bazookas at wide-eyed innocents in robes—I envied the interest he was able to work up in his companion.

He was not alone. All about us in the snow, those who had seen the film countless times already were lauding its endless merits to those who had who had not. Every cold cloud of breath was composed of heated reminiscences of *Star Wars*, dissipating and forming again till the converts near bounced, puppy dog style, in anticipation.

But try as I might, I could not excite my own companion. Despite my talk of Darth Vader, of Luke, of Obi-Wan, of the climactic air battle, there was no knocking the flirtatious redhead and her boyish looking best friend, whom we had met a few short nights ago, out of his head.

"They just live around the corner," he lamented-suggested. "It's like a block away."

I nodded indifferently, realizing that a battle much more fierce than the one between Skywalker and Vader was going on: me against my best friend, his raging teenage hormones versus my lust for the movie.

"You don't find it too cold in this line-up?" he battered away; faces all around us were, indeed, turning blue.

"Believe me," I replied, standing my wet ground, "it's worth it."

A long silence ensued, filled only by the nattering of the increasingly growing line, everyone eager to withstand the conditions in anticipation of the reward...everyone but my best friend.

"That's it!" he finally announced, declaring himself the winner and probably severing, he well knew, our friendship in the bargain. "I'm going."

Off he trundled, excusing himself from a long line of baffled faces, each member of which immediately categorized him an idiot, not only for turning his back on *Star Wars* but for doing so after having waited for so long in an ice-cold line-up.

Determined to prove that my interest was the greater, I stayed put. Slowly, the line advanced. Cheers rung out in the night air, and soon, the chorus of chattering teeth was replaced by an amplifying hum of anticipation.

I neared the box office. I was next...no. I would not be the next moviegoer. I would be the next idiot, bolting the line-up and running after my best friend...a bigger idiot than he, really, as I had made it as far as the cash.

A few minutes later, there I was, staring into a basement window at him. He was squeezed excitedly between the redhead and her equally vivacious companion.

I knocked on the window. All three heads, a single animal, looked up at me and burst into laughter.

"I told them you'd be here!" screamed my friend triumphantly. "Didn't I tell you?" he asked the girls. "There he is!"

"NO!" I announced, "I'm going home!"

And so, I did—no *Star Wars,* no girls. Neither of the sweet rewards—movies, sex—that were the staples of those years. Just a solitary figure, wandering home through the snow.

The moon, through the passages between the buildings, cut through downtown Ottawa like a light saber, severing the fantasists from the realists, the idiots from the smart, the connected from the disenfranchised.

☆☆☆☆☆

THAT AUGUST OF 1977, his posthumous presence plastered the planet: he was all over the news—clips from his films, excerpts from interviews, concert footage—but was just as visible on t-shirts, posters, and enough commemorative knickknacks to stock a gaggle of Gracelands.

A close friend of mine had just returned from Israel, where, she told me, young and old were mourning him too: Elvis.

My mother, estranged from my father for some years, cried like a teenager in the throes of her first break-up, replacing the curses she usually reserved for him with reminiscences of the tan-skinned pretty boy she first met to Elvis' earth-shattering music.

The National Enquirer—the only tabloid there was in those days—published a controversial front-page photo of the King in his coffin. The photo (the story came out later) was taken by a cousin of Elvis' on the take, a camera concealed in his tie pin. The public was outraged—but the Enquirer pleaded good corporate citizenship: "We gave the people what they wanted," they explained, "proof that the man was really gone."

It didn't work. Theories that Elvis remained alive and well lasted for the next fifteen years. In the end, of course, even the most stubborn of theorists was forced to say goodbye.

My goodbye took place to the sound of his greatest hits, as they blared across the crowded grounds of The Ex, the local summer fair. While exiting the premises with my girlfriend, I spotted a small photo in the left-hand corner of a newspaper some kid was hawking.

There it was, for only the squinting eye to see: Groucho Marx, dead at 87.

To have made that contribution to film, to television, to wit...only to be footnoted.

We reached our bus to the sounds of the musical tribute that had just started to climb the charts that week:

"The King is gone...the King is gone...but long live his name."

You bet your life.

✯✯✯✯✯

TONY BENNETT CROONED DUKE ELLINGTON, Bob Newhart stammered through some jokes, and an anonymous author in oversized glasses unrelentingly peddled a book.

It was called *The Best of Carson* but these were hardly the most prized items in the history of the *Tonight Show*—ho-hum enough, in fact, to prompt me to investigate other channels.

None of the other networks were faring much better: a rerun of *Kojak*, an episode from a discount horror series, and one of those boring foreign movies—some black and white thing about a kid with an oily crew cut and a sad expression.

Back to Johnny. A half-decent ad lib, a little banter with the band, then...then that kid with the crew cut again, with everything he said spelled under him...Why was I back here? What was it that was bringing me back to him, to such a "foreign," in so many ways, experience? Surely something bigger than boredom.

As I watched, I began to identify with him, began to recognize his world. Yes, it was black and white, and yes it was French (a language I had largely lost)...but too a world in which children—their energy, their confusion, their needs—are but annoyances in a melodramatically adult universe.

Paris, which I hitherto had only known as the Technicolor backdrop of overdone MGM musicals, framed this dilemma in an entirely different fashion: here, its oldness did not speak of romantic values, nor its arcane ornamentation of high art, nor its stony byways of over-the-top romantic rendezvous'.

The boy was trapped, cornered in this small, strange world, a world that—for all of the surface differences—paralleled mine with continued certainty: the philandering, neurotic mother... the taciturn, indifferent stepfather...the stern, self-righteous instructors.

Try as he might, he could not run away from it, any more than I could run away from my North American suburban version. He could only make it, as that famous final scene of

Truffaut's *The 400 Blows* affirmed, to a vast and daunting sea, to the edge, whose promises and possibilities he was probably just as unprepared for. The sweet suffocation of a redemptive future.

I turned the television off and retreated to the room I had in my mother's house. I lay awake, the resonant final close-up of the boy growing larger in my mind.

Soon, his was not just the face of a scarred and kindred spirit.

It was that of a flawed angel, showing me the way.

✯✯✯✯✯

"IS YOUR SISTER HOME?"

It was our neighbour, an attractive middle-aged brunette who often engaged my fifteen-year-old sister, who happened to be out with friends that night, to look after her newborn.

"Uh...no," I answered shyly.

"Oh," she smiled back. "Then I'm sure you can do it."

Do it? Do what?

The answer was to sit silently in their empty house while she and her husband slipped out.

Neighbourhood gossip had it that he was some all-important public face in the government. As such, this being Ottawa, they often found themselves at public functions. She, my mother had once whispered to me, was not his actual wife; he had a grown family somewhere on the West Coast. This was the woman with whom he shared a secret existence, in, smartly, a modest, pre-fabricated garden home indistinguishable from hundreds of other modest, pre-fabricated garden homes. They were hiding in plain sight.

I didn't let my face suggest that I knew any of this, that I was privy to the insiders' knowledge that I had just been asked to look after the living consequence of their clandestine coupling.

A twenty-dollar bill scratched hastily against the pocket of my shirt. "There'll be more later," she cooed, convinced that I had just been bought.

I hemmed and hawed until she took my hand.

"Come on," she insisted.

I entered their home. I was disappointed to find that in spite of their professional affluence, it was identical, in layout and décor, to ours.

"The baby's in the next room," she explained. "He'll sleep the whole time."

She'd better be right, I thought to myself, as I had never looked after a baby in my life. Then, without so much as another whisper of instruction, she was gone, off to join her missing husband.

Left to my devices, I began to look for clues about this "secret life" of theirs: a letter from the man's wife on the West Coast, filled with capital N naivete. Better still, one saying that she was finally wise to what was going on—and further, that she was fully prepared to expose his lies and to ruin his career.

Nothing. The only thing in the entire place suggesting the right mix of politics, romance and scandal was a copy of Margaret Trudeau's just published memoir.

I scanned the book here and there but found that even Margaret had no such titillation to offer.

Without the stimulation of either real-life melodrama or the baby violating his mother's behavioural predictions, I turned to the television.

I found a tall man with a bird-like walk, splitting his time between the joys of provincial domesticity and the weighty world of societal respectability.

Jacques Tati, as the contentedly silent Mr. Hulot, in *Mon Oncle*.

Between suppressed titters, for fear of waking up the baby, I began to understand whose home it was that I was in: people, like Hulot, who were enjoying the small life while they could, dodging, with less humour than he, the stultifying prospect of doing right by the world.

The film ended. The door opened. The woman, this time with husband, entered.

"See?" she whispered proudly, "I told you."

When she offered me the other twenty, I told her to keep it—but to call me anytime. I'd been brought to understand her, and to value the Tati-like silence that mercifully preserved her little life.

✰✰✰✰✰

I CAN SEE HER STILL, that bouncy, brown hair, that trim figure, those respectable legs under the hem of that baby blue uniform; you could steal a glimpse of them whenever she left her post to show some dowager the bath salts.

Had she ever noticed me, I wondered, that skinny, greasy-haired, infatuated teenager, in the store every day but never buying anything, only there to steal images of her, images I could take home and let run wild?

I doubt it. Any effort I sometimes made to get her to look at me—a too-loud cough, a carefully engineered moment of eye contact, a "casual" walk in front of her—always proved too modest...then again, it could be that every one of them registered and that she knew very well what I was up to, but that the cool friendliness she had to exhibit as part of her job was such a part of her now that there was no other mode of reaction. No finding my behavior cute, no being repulsed or brought to anger—nothing but that slightest of smiles, accommodating but just, just enough to get her through her day, just enough, perhaps, to get her through her life.

I never saw her in any other temperament, never saw her with the proverbial gloves off—except in my dreams, of course, where I saw her with everything off, sometimes the two of us making love right there in the store, rattling the countless tubes of shiny lipstick that surrounded her, toppling the packages of panty hose until they rained on top of us. Though she would definitely have to be the teacher—she was some ten years older than I, at least—in these fantasies, it was I who was in total control, pleasing her as no man—or boy—had, cracking the precious code of civility that entrapped her.

Finally, the stalemate was broken. One fateful afternoon, on my way, solo as usual, to the movies—a curiously premature revival of Mel Brooks' still young *Young Frankenstein*—who should be at the same bus stop? There she was, out of uniform, smoking, and in conversation with a friend—in all ways released from the bonds of professionalism.

I sat a few rows behind them on the bus and observed the back of her head as that billowy hair bounced, swished and flung about with every verbal volley between she and her companion.

To my amazement, she rang the bell just before I did. Could it be that she—that they—were going to this same movie?

Indeed they were. Again, I sat a few rows back and observed. No need to pay attention to the movie; I had seen it so many times I could recite the dialogue to the audience should the film break. No, contrary to my original plan for that afternoon, I was going to watch her. I sat enraptured as she wriggled from the last casings of her cocoon, as she tittered, snorted, and outright guffawed; dignity, at least for one afternoon, be damned! Thanks to the assistance of one of my then comic idols, she had come fully alive before my eyes, like Gene Wilder watching his creation do same.

Alas, she and her companion did not make the trip back with me. I was just sixteen and had no other life to go to. They, as young adults, had who knows: drinks in a bar somewhere, lunch at a nearby restaurant, maybe even—horror of horrors!—grown men to meet.

The next day, I returned to the drugstore where she worked...only to find that she wasn't there. Nor was she there the day after that, nor the day after that, nor...

Perhaps that was the cause of her raucous laughter in that theatre, her abandon. Funny as the film was, perhaps, to her, it wasn't that funny. Perhaps the film was merely the device by which she could celebrate her liberation from the bonds of propriety. Released at last, she was free to let it all out...and I, as a result, was free, sadly, of her.

That sixteen-year-old grew older and scoffed at populist film critic Roger Ebert. He called Everett Sloane's speech about an unconsumed infatuation with an anonymous woman the highlight of *Citizen Kane*. If that's the highlight, what the hell have you been looking at, Ebert?

Then, one day, after a long absence, the brunette from the drugstore made a comeback in his dreams.

He had been too hard, he then decided, on Ebert.

✰✰✰✰✰

FRANCOIS TRUFFAUT'S latest film had just opened. The critical word was that it was his best yet.

Sure, I could have seen it that night—but such was my zeal for his work that I had to see the first show, as in that afternoon, as in at The Somerset, as in instead of writing a Geography exam.

How to engineer this: the replacement of my academic obligation—for which I had barely studied anyway—with the experience of sitting alone in a darkened theatre in the exalted company of my favourite foreign filmmaker?

"It's my grandfather, sir," I began. "He's had a heart attack. Nobody quite knows what's going to happen. I have to go and see him. It might be my last chance."

The Geography teacher stared at me, a blank expression on

his face. I knew that, like all teachers, he had heard them all—and that he was well aware that I had shown no aptitude for his discipline and would therefore probably embarrass myself by writing this exam. "Well," he countered coolly, "you'll have to talk to the principal about this."

The principal? Oops! I didn't expect to land myself in *that* kind of trouble.

I had failed to pull the wool over the Geography teacher's eyes—and now I was expected to pull it over the principal's?

Still, this was Francois Truffaut at stake. It was worth a risk as sizeable as his talent.

I entered the principal's office. His ice blue eyes, through the small cloud of smoke created by the pipe he dramatically puffed, finally located me. "So," he began, "your grandfather." He'd been primed. "Yes, Sir." I answered. "Must be in pretty rough shape if you have to see him during an exam," he observed.

On and on I went, ad-libbing the way I typically blubbered before bullies, detail after horrifying detail. My climax: the doctors—what doctors?—had told my mother he might have mere minutes, no, make that seconds, to live.

"Well," the principal continued philosophically, priming his curve, "death is a funny thing. You never know. Could be taking a turn for the better right now. Could be chasing nurses as we speak."

Chasing nurses? Jesus! Had my story been *that* unconvincing? "Why don't we call the hospital, see how he's doing," he suggested.

"Unfortunately," I faked, continuing to play muse to my ruse, "I don't know the room number."

"Somebody does. Your mother for example." With that, he began to dial my mother's work number.

I was sunk. Despite giving it my all, he had bested me. The Establishment wins again!, I lamented—until, much to our mutual surprise, tears the size of matured chestnuts began streaming down my face. Surprising me still, they continued, unstoppably, until my cheeks were shiny with them. As a result, he began to think that perhaps I was telling the truth. To affirm it, though, he handed me the phone.

"You talk to her." As in, if this is real and I'm about to play hard-ass with a woman on the brink of losing her father, that's a public relations disaster.

"Hi, Mom," I began, then went on, converting my still falling tears to audible form, until finally, she asked me what was wrong. "*Pepère*," I offered quietly, "is he still in the hospital? Is he going to pull through?"

She was sly enough herself to recognize exactly what I was up to; it was the kind of a con worthy of the woman to whom I was speaking, she of the extra-marital affairs and the can't-go-to-work-today hangovers.

"You've got something you want to get out of, don't you, Danny," she deduced. "Uh huh," I offered humbly. "And you're crying? In front of somebody important?"

I gave her the same uh huh again. "Oh son," she said proudly, cognizant for some time now of my showbiz aspirations. "You'll make such a good actor."

I got out of the exam and saw the movie.

A full decade after I left that school, it became the city's first high school for the performing arts.

I'd like to think I set the precedent.

✯✯✯✯✯

"WE HAVE a history of meeting at bus stops." I laughed. I had forgotten.

The film was *Young Frankenstein*. I had seen it many times in its initial release but here it was, a mere three years later, playing again at downtown's Nelson.

There was a lot at stake that afternoon. If she laughed at the same things I did, then I'd know that this was it, the thing I had been desperately looking for ever since I had first discovered girls, something with potential to grow, something beyond the nervous handholding, the flirtatious comment, or those other junior high school mating rituals.

After the film, from which we both emerged still laughing (yes!), she introduced me to her favourite Baskin-Robbins flavours, chocolate mint and peanut butter and chocolate, a combination I still order whenever I guiltily indulge.

I sat on the dewy green, enjoying the last of my ice cream and basking in the site of her turning expert cartwheels. A few stared. Regardless, she carried blissfully on. The indifference inherent in her happiness became as much a part of the attraction for me as her surrender to the jokes in the film.

Finally, some four hours after we had set out that sunny Saturday, some two weeks after we had chance-encountered at a bus stop, there we were, again awaiting public transportation. Her bus arrived, and, as part of the goodbye, I enjoyed my first kiss of consequence.

That moment was still there between us, I'd like to think, that day just last week, when we set eyes on each other for the first time in almost thirty years.

Instead of movie dialogue and ice cream, there was small talk —her sons, my daughter...her husband, my wife...her parents, both living...my parents, both gone—and sushi.

When her bus arrived, I was a little sorry that we could not, in a fit of synchronized nostalgia, recreate the big finish that had climaxed what had been the first ever date for either of us, all those years ago.

I watched the bus whisk her to the same suburb in which she had grown up, then walked to my intended destination in the rain.

Young no more.

✯✯✯✯✯

"I SAW this great movie last night."

He, one of my closest friends, didn't go to the movies. "You wanna go?" But this one, whatever it was, he not only saw, he wanted to see again.

We grabbed a bite to eat and ambled in the Saturday afternoon sunshine to the Capitol Square.

"Hey." The door wasn't giving. He pulled again. "What the hell...?" We both stepped back, had a look at the marquee, the one that was supposed to read *All that Jazz*. What it read was, "Closed Due to Projectionists' Strike."

"Oh well", he shrugged. Despite the rare show of enthusiasm he had initially demonstrated, he was perfectly nonplussed. Sure, easy for him. His real haunts were arcades. He had Pacman, Tetrus, and Berserk. I had...nothing.

A projectionists' strike—despite years of movie going, I had no idea that such a thing could even happen—and this, the summer of so much choice fare.

What was to become of me? My whole life revolved around the tiny circuit of Ottawa's cinemas. It's where I went to escape my feuding family, where I took girls, where I secretly rendezvous'd with my estranged father, the man unpaid child support decreed I was not supposed to see.

And hey, I had even landed my first job. Me, in show business, at last! I played a singing Muskox (yes, a singing Muskox) in a production for The Museum of Nature. What would I blow my cash on?

Buses was the answer, the ones I took every second weekend to Montreal, where dedicated projectionists dutifully loaded reels of film. In one day—one day!—I caught *The Empire Strikes Back, The Shining, The Blues Brothers,* and a contraband print of Hitchcock's *Rear Window*.

On the ride home, I would relive each scene of each film,

mortally terrified that my memory might, before strike's end, grow improbably dim.

Come fall, the strike ended. Ottawa could go to the movies again. I made it a prideful habit of advising people on what and what not to go see. After all, I had seen it all—with one dutiful exception.

"Great movie, huh?" my friend commented, as, a full season after we had first headed out, we emerged from the Capitol Square. So, he was a devotee after all, cementing us forever.

Movies, that summer had taught me, weren't the only things to be prized.

✫✫✫✫✫

WHY HAD I STOPPED GOING? Or perhaps the question was, why was I going now, after—what had it been?—ten years?

Guilt, that quality the Catholic faith, the one whose symbols made up the decorating scheme of his tiny, first floor apartment, had so deeply instilled in me?

Or maybe just the sudden realization that each visit now—the man was pushing eighty—might be the last?

Baseball? Hmm. Maybe. After all, he was the one who had introduced me—a preschooler visiting his LeBreton Flats home at the time—to the game.

When I suggested, after the long silences between us that had begun our awkward afternoon together, that we turn the set to Pete Rose and company taking on our beloved Expos, he was —Eureka!—all smiles. By the second inning, however, his wrinkled face had grown sullen. "There's a lot of blacks who play the game today, huh? I don't like that." Rose made a nice play in the fourth. It was evident that with this kind of defense, the game was already in the visitors' bag. By the fifth, we were talking about the industry whose ladder I was soon hoping to climb. "There's a lot of Jews in the movie business, isn't there? I don't like that." By the seventh, after a George Foster dinger, there was something that I didn't like: the imminent possibility of another "I don't like that." By the eighth, like Montreal's hapless starter, I was out of there.

I tried one last time before he died. What on earth possessed me to choose the movies as a bonding agent I still don't know—particularly as mention of them had revealed his anti-Semitism. But this visit, I stubbornly convinced myself, would be different. After all, it was a Western. No, the Western: *High Noon*. In its tight-lipped, self-made hero who finds no aid in his community—a parallel to his own circumstance raising four children by himself—Pepère, I was sure, would find the kind of personality he could tolerate, and I, finally would enjoy our time together.

On the surface, it was another typical meeting between us; words were exchanged with the same economy as Gary Cooper's pattern of speech. But as the film rolled on, the evening became different. As Coop rendez-vous'd with destiny, it became evident that a mutual interest was at last taking hold. We were joined at the giddy, disproportionate feeling only the movies can provide, both full of that special inner momentum, the kind that dispenses barriers the way Coop was—bang!, bang!, bang!—dispensing with the notorious Miller gang. Will Kane, Coop's character, had done in an hour and a half what nothing else, over a period many years, could.

Weeks later, my thoughts returned to the film's setting, Hadleyville, when my grandfather's lifeless body was climactically committed, like Will Kane's marshal's badge, to the dust.

☆☆☆☆☆

WHAT THE HELL IS THIS?

I can't make head or tail out of it!

First, those big, bold abbreviations, EXT and INT—whatever those mean. And those constant CUT TOs that keep cropping up. And those annoying "we see, we see"s all over the place. Then, those bare bones descriptions of the characters, only vaguely conveying their wit, charm or foolish courage.

Those names and that dialogue that don't come at you left to right, the way those plays I take out of the library do. Why are they all centered? Worst of all, those big, blocky passages standing in for the heart pounding chases and the suspenseful gun play, the stuff that almost made me break my seat at the theatre (the Nelson) when my aunt took me, now replaced by all of these ideas about sound and cameras and music?

How the hell am I going to write something like this? If this is what *Butch Cassidy and the Sundance Kid* had to look like before it became *Butch Cassidy and the Sundance Kid*, I'm never going to be able to do it. Some spy wrote this, in some kind of code, or some technical guy maybe, for other technical guys. Is this honestly what writers give to actors and directors? What they win Academy Awards for?

Curse this goddamn paperback! Now there's this huge divide between me and my life's purpose. Suddenly, I'm forced, like Butch and Sundance, to high tail it to some place where I can think this all out, where I can figure out some way to do what I'm supposed to do despite being threatened.

It's going to be tough, though. After all, they had a plan B. It's written out right here, in the middle of the book, just before the pictures (thank God for the pictures, which do remind me of the movie): Bolivia, that middle part where Butch and Sundance escape from the surprise posse.

But there's no Bolivia in my life, at least, not yet—no Plan B, nothing other than getting through high school and finding my way, by a miracle that has yet to be figured out, to California, with a suitcase full of brilliant scripts that have yet to be figured out either.

What's this on the last page? They don't even write "The

End." They put two different words there: "Fade out." Oh—I see, like on page one, where it says "Fade In." Ah! I get it!

Oh—and "Ext" must be "Exterior." I guess you have to tell the production people where you are. So they'll know where to show up when they film it. And "Int.", that must be "Interior"...

Hmm...

☆☆☆☆☆

"MY GOD!" she reflected. "I would see you with that thing, in the snow..."

"That thing" was a typewriter, in that last, primitive age before the advent of computers, which I would rent with money I had saved by skimping on what I had been given by my father to buy my lunch at school.

In my arms, however, it felt like a battleship, an analogy fostered by its ugly gun metal carapace and its taxing effect on my hopelessly underdeveloped arms. Regardless, I would carry this prized conduit between myself and fame and fortune all the way from the smallish Bank Street shop from which I had procured it to the Alta-Vista-based apartment that I shared with my father and grandmother.

I didn't know it at the time but my beloved grandmother was standing at the window on these occasions, a maternal eye on that small, struggling dot in the strip mall parking lot across the way, desperately negotiating its wintry surface.

Once inside, she would mercifully re-inflate my sagging form with a rejuvenating bowl of warm, homemade soup. Then, I'd get cracking, my forefingers busily committing the latest movie idea I was certain would show the world I was a young, undiscovered genius to paper. Its unquestioned production would rescue me from a life of high school bullies, shoplifting, and struggles with the opposite sex.

Much to my chagrin, however, each of these scripts ended up

no more than pale imitations of something I had just seen—a realization that would always kick in at about page twenty.

At that point, I would silently stew, until, succumbing to frustration entirely, I would venture to the nearby garbage chute and send my weekend's work for a long, rattling ride into a foul-smelling vortex. Then, I'd return to the apartment, lift up the typewriter, and bring it back by bus to its rightful home, vowing, with each throb of my pipe cleaner arms, never to attempt to write again.

But there I'd be, a few weekends later, back at the rental shop, desperate to commit something in the tradition of the latest comedy or blockbuster to print.

"I used to think you were crazy," Memère continued, many years later. "But now..." "Now": staff writer for a highly rated animated series (*The Raccoons*), my first bona fide industry credit. "Now I say to myself," a drag on her cigarette, "he wasn't crazy after all."

No, not crazy. But on days when the ideas don't flow, my arms act up.

☆☆☆☆☆

"I'LL NEVER WRITE AGAIN!"

The words were inspired by a notebook whose pages were filled with my smallish handwriting. I had just snatched it from his hands.

"Don't be ridiculous," he answered. His voice had taken on the cool of a lion tamer placating a particularly put-out beast.

I wanted to dig my claws into the pages, into him—my own father—for their failure as agents of the obvious: the fact that I was a natural, a boy wonder, an eighteen-year-old who wrote with the insight, wit, and technical prowess of a man of forty.

He talked some more, though I couldn't hear him through the shell of my wound, until I bid him a diplomatic goodbye—it was all I could offer as reconciliation. I boarded the bus back to my mother's. She'd be holding a drink in her hands when I got home, complaining about how the booze was burning a small hole in her chest. For the first time ever, I would know how she felt.

How tempting it was to liberate each page from their soft-muscled captors, the flimsy metal rings that confined them to narrative coherence, and to let the wind that was whipping in and out of the bus window do with them what it would. I could see them populating Bank Street, like paper pigeons, fluttering between the businesses, somebody else's problem now.

But I didn't do it.

I got home, bid my mother hello, went up to my room. I examined the white pages of my script, and held each one with a mix of tenderness, pain and resolve—like Marlon Brando in *On the Waterfront*, cradling his dead pigeons. Okay then, you can hear him resolving behind his eyes, now I know the true scale of what it is I'm up against.

I put the notebook in a bottom drawer, then sat down to write. I paused, rose, let the drawer out just an inch or two. I wanted it, my father's eye, to see me, see me write and write and write and write. I wrote remembering the final images of Kazan's film: post-pigeon Brando, bruises and blood...triumphant.

☆☆☆☆☆

WE WOULD WRESTLE—SOMETIMES, in the unlikeliest of places.

Our most memorable match—the one we still laugh about—took place in his bedroom, situated in a low-rent, high-rise a half-mile from the city post office. Depressed over his recent break-up, he could not be coerced from bed. His mother, who had endured this for some time, said to me: "I'm beginning to think he's given up on girls altogether."

I bounced on the mattress till a pink, tussle-haired bundle emerged from the swaddle of sheets. Despite his depression-based lethargy, in no time, there were gales of laughter, and, inevitably, a boyish bout of wrestling. That, of course, is when his mother, more and more convinced that her son was considering substitutes for the opposite sex, walked into the room, the two of us atop one another thanks to a particularly involved leg hold.

Needless to say, there weren't too many more impromptu wrestling matches after that...until the wall.

The wall was a waist-high brick barrier separating the apartment building from a strip mall. That fateful evening, I had just coerced this friend of mine, never much of a moviegoer, to accompanying me to the latest Gene Wilder comedy at The Place de Ville. When he began to change his mind, a wrestling match ensued. Though I weighed all of ninety pounds, I somehow managed to push him off the aforementioned wall—and on to that safest of landings: his right knee.

I didn't spend that evening with Gene Wilder—unless Gene was quietly patrolling the halls of the Ottawa General Hospital. When my friend emerged from some back room in an obviously uncomfortable cast, I tried to make light of it all. Inside, however, I began to ponder, for the first time in my life, the depth of my attachment to the movies—specifically, the extremes that it was capable of driving me to.

Semi-sourly, some twenty-five years later, my friend said to me, "Listen to this, pal," and began to bend his right knee for me. With each application of pressure, his knee made a sound like a strongman squeezing an empty bottle of Evian. The excruciating discomfort, the sleepless nights, and the failed therapies were explained to me in full detail. An operation was imminent, brought on by "a history of previous injury."

After a quarter century's absence, my guilt over my love of movies had returned.

The next time we met—a year or so later—my friend had acquired a number of equipotent, if contrasting, interests: religion and bodybuilding. The latter he took special pride in. Most of the expected dinner conversation, in fact, was replaced by proud flexes of his oak-like arms, his beefy shoulders, his protruding pecs. When he began to brag about how many pounds he could lift over his head, I commented, "Uh...I assume your knee is all better." "Oh," he offered, "my knee was cured by the Lord a year ago"—then proceeded to make his calves pop out.

The Lord, then, had bagged himself a two-for-one deal, removing both my friend's pain and, at long last, my guilt, allowing me to fully enjoy the movies again.

✯✯✯✯✯

"*FRANKENSTEIN*, Y'EVER SEE *FRANKENSTEIN*?"

Of course I had, and all of his other favourites too: *Dracula, The Mummy,* Universal's entire stockpile of spooks. As he lovingly poured over every still frame in his book, the coffee table translation of the James Whale classic, his eyes, even though he had probably indulged in this ritual a hundred times, visibly glossed over. I was nestled over his shoulder—it was a narrow booth, a downtown parking lot's—watching him turn the pages with his one good arm.

What had happened to the other, the one that stopped at the elbow? Close as we became over the brief period that we worked together, I never asked. Was that, I started to ponder after endless conversations about movie monsters, what was responsible for his love of Karloff, Lugosi, and Chaney? Did he honestly see himself as their brethren, a physical anomaly, an outcast, a tortured soul? And if so, who was I to him: the scientist who recognized his innate goodness? The sympathetic blind man to whom the physical meant nothing? The understanding but helpless cop who bore witness to his torments?

The day he was fired—I can't recall the reason but I remain certain it was trivial—he cried. Teary, he deftly packed up his movie books with his good arm, secured them against his ribs in order to free his one good hand, and bade me goodbye. The next day, though I desperately needed the small salary, I quit in solidarity.

When next we encountered—some fifteen years later, a public place—I didn't recognize him. He was half obscured from me, nestled against a girl I knew. She introduced him as her new boyfriend. I extended my hand. Nothing. "Geez, you sure you want to be with a guy like this?" I cracked. "Talk about anti-social!" The combination of her tense smile and the full revelation of his being let me know just how big a faux pas I had committed. I had not only embarrassed the three of us, I had destroyed the possibility of being able to express how glad I was to see him again. He nodded sullenly. I retreated to my seat. Did he recognize me but was now ashamed to know me, or had he really forgotten who I was? It couldn't be the latter. It was Me! Me, the scientist who understood him, the blind man who had bonded with him, the cop who had cared.

In time, Frankenstein, Dracula, and The Mummy were replaced, on screen, by mental patients in hockey masks. They didn't look for kindness or friendship or any other form of solidarity.

And they could kill with just a stare.

☆☆☆☆☆

SHE WAS big boned (by her own admission) and fresh-faced, her trademark attire jeans and matching jacket. But here she was, at his place for the weekend, in black dress, stockings, and full make-up, if chancily applied. "You look like a five-dollar hooker!" he pronounced. Tears streamed down her cheeks, leaving trails of mascara that weaved like downtown derelicts.

The elevator door opened. I came face to sullied face with her. "What happened?" She fell into my arms and sobbed some more. I led the both of us back into the elevator, and, after its door cut us off from the tenth floor of the downtown Y, we simply stood there. At last, she separated from my shoulder and spoke.

She told me the whole story: how she had lied to her family, telling them that she'd be staying at a girlfriend's, but the plan, of course, was to stay with him, my best friend, the one I had dropped by to see on my way to a revival of Chaplin's *The Gold Rush*. Her attempt to make herself look sexy for him was such a failure, though, that after his hooker comment, he had gone so far as to toss her out. "I can't go back to my parents' place now," she wailed. "Can you help me find a place to stay?"

The film was slated to begin in an hour. All morning I had been anticipating it, like a kid awaiting Christmas. Could we get this done before it began? Find her an affordable motel room, determine the future of their relationship, and say our diplomatic goodbyes?

We did it, astonishingly, in half the time. Before I knew it, there she sat on the bed of a barely respectable downtown hotel, complacent as could be. "You deserve a reward for this," she laughed, relieved. "Where did you say you were going?"

With that, she took my hand…and led me to the bed.

A mere hour after I had set foot on the main lobby of the Y, there I was, in the dark of the theatre, a virgin no longer, sitting through Chaplin's *The Gold Rush*.

I left the screening sober faced. The whole film struck me as childish.

ACT THREE

I WAS A GENIUS.

At least, during the honeymoon period over which we first got to know each other.

After all, I was some ten years younger and a high school drop-out, and yet, when it came to wisecracking, I could rattle off enough bon mots to crowd a bowl of alphabet soup.

Occasionally even, the synchronized cackle I could elicit from the pair of them—these two self-made twenty-somethings who had just rescued me from a life as a teenage stand-up to write radio commercials for their fledgling company—could be so high pitched and so long as to emulate a crate of unhappy chickens—a sound I had never even heard from those dark, anonymous hordes to which I had been prostituting my golden wit between acts at a local folk club.

I was an inexhaustible source to them, a deep comic gold mine—one they were sure they could excavate for a long, long time. And for the time being at least, I was happy to be stripped, little by little, of the marrow of my funny bone, for I knew there was plenty more where that came from—that the depths of my talents were more vast than even they, with their eye for a hot creative property, could imagine.

I was certain, too—for I had heard it suggested in bits and pieces—that whenever I left their offices, that they were exchanging "Wows!" and "Incredible!"s and "Where the hell did that kid come from?"s, and classifying me as a Neil Simon or even—on a smokin' hot day—a Mark Twain in the making.

There was probably even some afterthought that revealed their deepest greed, like, "Let's get what we can out of this kid before we lose him—because we're going to."

One morning, I negotiated the coffee-coloured shag rug that lined the offices and met my companions with the usual anticipation.

"So," I offered confidently, "What are we going to apply ourselves to today?" At which point, normally, the day's assignments would be related to me—clients included a jean outlet, an optician's, and the place where we occasionally ate lunch—and we would start the process: the banter back and forth whose purported purpose was to come up with thirty seconds of radio comedically so memorable that it instantly put the client's name on everybody's tongue, but whose real intention was simply to make one another laugh—on a good day, till we wet our pants.

Instead, what I got was a somber, "I saw you on Bank Street last night"—the main drag—from the easiest of the two laughers, and a look that told me at once that a page had turned, a big page, and that he now saw me in a completely different light. "You were cruising for newspapers."

And indeed I had been—for that was how I spent my evenings, leaving my father, suffering from his extended mid-life crisis, to our welfare-subsidized apartment, to travel from public trash can to public trash can, looking for the national newspapers that I could not—despite the radio salary—afford, in order to comb them for every scrap they had on anything entertainment, from jokes and puff pieces to film reviews and interviews.

But I had been spotted and the word was out: I was no boy wonder, who had formed genie-like out of the dust of some great joke book. There was a life behind the wit, one of penury, of loneliness, and of a desperate search to belong to a more legitimate and glamourous world.

The pedestal had cracked, and all inter office triumphs from now would be made up of a laughter that was, at least in part, noticeably hollow.

I remembered the folk clubs, and the wonderful darkness that cloaked you.

✫✫✫✫✫

I CAME into the office with a gait that belied my one hundred and thirty-five pounds.

Every step I took resulted in large impressions on the rug, attributable to the incongruous lumber of my tread.

My co-workers—we all wrote ad copy together…that is, when we weren't busy stepping out to play video games, enjoying long, ethnic lunches or shopping for vintage clothing—momentarily wondered what gave. Finally, the wind chime-like symphony from my pockets added a tell-tale detail.

"What are you doing with all that change?" one of them asked.

I explained:

That afternoon—in those days just before the invention of the VCR—a Buster Keaton film I was dying to see, *The Three Ages*, was scheduled to play on French television.

As I couldn't go home for lunch and still call it a productive—or in the tradition of that particular office, acceptably semi-productive—day, I would spend my laissez-faire lunch hour at the bus station. There, for those forced to endure long wait times for that precious, crammed ride to, say, North Bay, were uncomfortable plastic chairs with built-in television sets. One quarter would buy you five minutes. Hence, two hours—the Keaton film plus commercials—equaled sixteen quarters, the tiny, circular musical instruments that had been playing in my pockets.

My co-workers thought I was nuts. What kind of a character would go to that length to watch some stupid, obscure silent movie? I rebutted by pointing out their individual bents: one's costly love of Matchbox cars, the other's disposition toward ill-fitting bicycle shorts. I remained, however, a creature of lesser standing.

Though I desperately sought the approval of these two in all things—I was, after all, their junior by some seven years—the prospect of soon seeing Keaton's *Three Ages* imbued me with enough inner confidence to risk their estimation.

At the allotted hour, I excused myself from our tiny office and jingled confidently through the downtown streets, reaching at last that poor man's Bijou, the Catherine Street Bus Terminal.

I settled into one of the less than accommodating chairs, waited 'til exactly the right moment, then, inserted my sixteen quarters into the slot.

The television flickered. It flickered again. For a moment, I panicked. Then, finally, the set came dutifully to life, alive with the much-anticipated image of...Anwar Sadat, as he collapsed at the hands of his own troops.

There was an immediate cut to studio, where French politicos just as deadpan but nowhere near as entertaining as Buster Keaton pontificated, pontificated and—goodbye, last of my quarters!—pontificated.

I stormed back to the office, my feet no longer prompting a jingling sound but the heavy stamp of an angry young man.

"So...,"one of the guys asked, his eyes on some copy for some stereo store, "how was your precious movie?"

No response. He looked up at me.

It was I who had spent all of that hard-earned change...but it was he who got to see The Great Stone Face.

✰✰✰✰✰

THAT HOLE in the ozone layer—could it have been the work of just two men?

I often wonder how much ground we covered, all those nights in his car, circling the city, talking movies.

He couldn't do it anywhere else, couldn't talk over pizza in a restaurant or from a comfy chair in either of our living rooms. It had to be the road.

Then again, he was a salesman. That's where he spent most of his reflective time, going over what to say, how to say it, what words might win he and his wife their next meal: a whole life in a car. So, if that was his special thinking spot, then that, when it came to sharing our taste in movies, was where it would be shared.

It was mostly comedies, the verbal, neurotic sort that populated the era into which he came of age, in the working-class enclave of Scranton, Pennsylvania—films I caught later, on TV, in the squeakier setting of suburban Montreal.

We talked Alan Arkin, Charles Grodin, George Segal, and a handful of others—any character who, like him, had shun the Old Order's way to happiness and was desperately looking to put their house in order according to a new, entirely improvised plan, with wit the only recourse when, more often than not, things failed.

We would recite our favourite lines, a Neil Simon here, a Carl Reiner there, and crack each other up, wearing down his tires all the while.

Curiously, we only ventured to the movies together once, when the pleasure he took in the few things he considered beneath him, like discount production values and limited acting ability, inspired him to take me to the Britannia Drive-in to catch Lou Ferrigno as *Hercules*. We snacked on licorice bits, and every time something particularly ill-produced arose, he'd throw his head back in a welcome convulsion, exhibiting a tongue as black as the many roads we had travelled.

We were still talking movies on his death bed—a makeshift one set up in his living room—when his face was thin and green with cancer. The heavy morphine he was on was seriously depriving him of his trademark brio, but it wasn't enough to rob him of the joy he got from the remembrance of a choice comic line, for which he'd come fully alive.

The last I saw of him was when his coffin, after his well-attended funeral, was loaded into a hearse. The hearse turned the corner...and I never saw him again.

But...I never saw the hearse stop anywhere either.

I trust it's still on the road somewhere, and that, thanks to some inexplicable miracle, he has managed to spring back to life, is sitting up in his coffin, and is exchanging funny lines with the movie-loving driver.

✰✰✰✰✰

As I write these words, with but my faster-than-the-human-eye right index finger, a ballpoint pen is in my left hand, squeezed between my thumb and forefinger. The forefinger nervously presses it against the thin flesh surrounding the left side of the thumbnail, activating a small, dull pain. The pen, as a result, looks like a tiny windshield wiper in accelerated motion. This idiosyncratic gesture allows me, somehow, to process, to figure out which idea, in which words, comes next.

This tick is activating, I've read, the right side of my brain, the creative side. Bereft of pen, I'm Julius Epstein without his brother, Billy Wilder without I.A.L. Diamond, Norman Panama without Melvin Frank.

It's the miniaturization of a more obvious impulse. As a child, crafting never-to-be-seen screen stories on the walk home from school, it was sticks; as a young man, less dangerously and slightly more acceptably, plastic coat hangers; in maturity, hoping to cloak this lifelong habit in sophistication, a riding crop.

One New Year's Eve, though, it was a cane—a late Christmas

gift lovingly presented to me by a woman magnetized by my poetic qualities yet uncomfortable with my romantic affections. It was handmade, shiningly lacquered, and presented with the same love with which it had been crafted. With this acceptable icon of social eccentricity, she was both gilding my habit and hoping to cure me of its incongruity.

Unsure that I could replace my precious, hand-friendly co-scenarists with this large and practical one, I tested it. Out into the streets I ventured, the snow blanketing Ottawa Centre unsullied by footprints. All on this night, at this time, were in homes, in clubs, in convention centres, readying for the coming hour that would tip us into the second installment of the Eighties.

The world, then, was an empty stage, on which I could perform to my heart's delight. Thus cued, I improvised story after story, converting the cane, which felt ever strange and heavy in my hand, to props from lances to light sabers. In the end, though, nothing held. My mind remained as unimprinted as the snow.

I walked back to the unrequited one's apartment, shouted "Happy New Year!" and presented her with a gift of my own: the cane.

Interesting as it was, I explained, there was nothing really special in it. The cane to me was what I was to her.

☆☆☆☆☆

THE RAVEN black hair that bounced in rhythm to her low-key cool...the lithe, mature whisper by which she was expressing herself...those long, elegant legs, the ones that moved about in service of some flimsy agenda I can't recall, torturing me.

Overwhelmed by it all...I ejaculated.

"What were you thinking about?" she asked—and not the beauty who'd been mesmerizing me from the screen. My girlfriend, the one whose head, all that time, had been busily bobbing.

"You," I, of course, lied.

We left the theatre, had a bite to eat. We conversed—books, friends, current events—while I probed her eyes for some sense that she was on to me, that she knew that it was not her talents alone that gotten things done; that there had been an accomplice.

Nothing. Those eyes were as pure as the spring water she was drinking.

By evening's end, as I walked her to her apartment just off the Rideau Canal, all was as it had ever been. I knew it by her traditional sign-off: a passionate kiss, a squeeze of the hand, and that sweet, innocent smile—the combination by which she assured me that her love for me was incorruptible, her faith complete.

Still…I never got sex in a movie theatre again.

She went on to a happy life, one that included a solid career.

The glamour girl didn't fare as well.

She made a fatal Hollywood mistake. She hadn't slept with the producer or the director.

She had slept with the audience.

☆☆☆☆☆

"WHAT ARE you two up to in there?" he would ask, knowing full well that whatever it was, it was yet another scene out of a French movie.

Jules and Jim, specifically, which I had discovered a few short years before. And if this, the two of us sharing the same woman, was not exactly as spirited, complicated or tragic as that, it remained the closest I was going to come to living out what Truffaut had put up on the screen.

Lately, however, he had begun to grow uncomfortable with

the whole idea. Unlike myself or the woman we shared, he was no French film lover and so jealousy, or guilt or, could it be?, love, had begun to well up inside of him.

She would have liked it to have been exactly that, for him to devote himself to her with totality. But, loyal as he was, that kind of commitment was out of the question. And so, somewhere, somehow, a triangle formed.

Neither of we males, to our credit, thought the lesser of her for the sharing. He was happy that she no longer had excuses to announce that her life was unfulfilled. I was happy that she didn't sell herself short by settling only for the functional. And she was the happiest of all, happy that all versions of her—from the meat-and-potatoes country girl to the closet intellectual—was at last satisfied.

There was nothing as crazy as dressing her up in men's clothes, as chilling as her threatening us with vitriol, as shocking as she driving us all off of a pier, as at the end of the film. The whole thing operated on a diplomatic understanding: that true friends shared everything.

Until, of course, the comments began, like a critic growing frustrated with the liberalism of French films.

And so, the relationship grew to a foursome. Our new partner was morality. I was the first to couple with it, deciding that the arrangement had to end. But how? By distancing myself from them? I was too in like with him for that, too in love with her. By making her my own? Maybe, but that meant the loss of him in the bargain. By leaving it for his increasing discomfort to decide? Perhaps, but that implied either involuntary banishment or perpetual suffering of the sight of them as a couple.

Like Jules and Jim, then, I would let the woman decide.

A few months later, she did, first severing ties with me, then, more heatedly, with him.

We grieved together he and I, particularly when word came that she was seeing someone else.

Yes, we had all jumped from the car, but she first, while safety was still in sight.

For my friend and I, it was a long and difficult swim. We were wet for weeks.

☆☆☆☆☆

Do you know why Nancy Reagan had a black baby?

I don't. And odds are good I never will.

The set up was all I could make out. I knew French, and figured hey, if you're familiar with one romantic language, you know them all. But whatever the punch line to this joke was, way back in 1986, I couldn't figure it out, regardless of how many times I squinted at the words through the midday Spanish sun.

I had seen much during this first-ever trip to Europe, subsidized by freelance advertising work, but this intrigued me as much as anything.

The jokes were printed on a placard outside a nightclub in the heart of Barcelona, a plug for Spain's number one film and stage comedian, a little man with a large mustache who would not have been out of place in a silent comedy. The jokes, judging by my limited grasp of the tongue, were topical and saucy—but if I couldn't make out the punch lines, I figured, I'd be better off finding my laughs somewhere else.

Sure enough, they were keeping themselves just a few blocks away, where a local cinema was playing a well-worn copy of a film I had seen many times: *Golfus De Roma,* better known as *A Funny Thing Happened on the Way to the Forum.* This'll work, I thought; my familiarity with the jokes is such that language definitely won't be a barrier.

Besides, this movie is so choc-a-block with mugs, pratfalls, visual gags, and manic cutting that the verbal is almost superfluous—plus, there are the songs, those witty Sondheim songs I so fell in love with upon first seeing the film. I've seen these dubbed these pictures before, I reminded myself. They never mess with the songs. Too hard to translate.

I settled into my seat. The overture began, and into frame appeared that lovable schizo, Zero Mostel. "Comedy Tonight!" he promised...in—what was this?—Spanish?

Even the songs?...oh well. *Golfús De Roma,* in toto, it would have to be.

Fortunately, I was right about the diversity of the content, and walked away more than happy, humming the film's melodies if not the lyrics and still-framing the prize expressions on Mostel's versatile visage.

As I neared my hotel, I spotted it again, that sign:

Do you know why Nancy Reagan had a black baby?

No. I don't. And if I did, I'm sure that I wouldn't find it funny. The real humor, I now knew, the stuff that lasts, operates on a plane above topicality and language.

And it's not in Spain either. It's in Rome.

✩✩✩✩✩

"So," I asked him, "What possessed you to join the army?"

We were tramping through Europe, and I was trying to fall into the rhythm of his steps. "Are you kiddin' me?" he answered. "That's John Wayne shit. I always wanted to do John Wayne shit."

Up to that point, I was certain that the generations whose heads had been turned by the exploits of The Duke had either grown old and died or gone to WW2 or Vietnam and died. But here it was, two decades post the latter conflict, and this tall, curly-topped twenty-five-year-old was still listing John Wayne as his life's inspiration.

"Come on, High-Speed"—he called everybody, and everything, he liked "High-speed." In the mechanically savvy environment in which he kept company, "high speed" was, well, high praise. "Try and keep up."

I smiled and walked a little faster. We were traversing Barcelona, en route to the train station. He had decided the manner in which we were going to part company, four days after our chance meeting: he would leave for North Africa.

"Why North Africa?" I asked, with the same Sancho Panzian respect I had used asking about the army. "I don't know," he answered with his usual cool. "It's just a place I've never been before."

We walked some more. Eager to jar more "why this's" and "why that's" from me I guess, he dramatically broke the silence:

"I killed a guy once." Just like that, just like "John Wayne shit" or "Never been before." "Really?" I marvelled, my Canadianess showing through in my absolute devastation over this all-American confession. "Yeah. We were told to go into this hut and retrieve some dead rangers." Grenada. It's a trivia question now, was a very big deal then. "There were no dead rangers in that hut. It was a secret ammo hut. They were snipers in the trees. I got one. The guys were all impressed. They were like, 'Man, you got a confirmed kill.'"

He got ahead of me. A sunbeam hit him, and yes, for a moment, I did see John Wayne.

"I think about him sometimes. Maybe he had a girlfriend, maybe he liked soccer..." The light changed. No. Not like John Wayne.

"See this?" He brought one of his big, long hands to his sweaty forehead and swept back some grapevine-shaped curls, revealing an ugly faintness. "What's that?" I was getting very good at this stooge thing. "Guy threw a grenade right in front of me. I had just enough time to look down and say 'Shit!' Boom!" I gulped. "They sent me home. I threw up all day for a week. They had to buff it of, the damage. The needles hurt worse than the grenade. I got them everywhere: under the eyes, in the temples..."

Where were those scenes, I wondered, in all of those John Wayne movies? Where was the throwing up at home scene and the needles to the boniest parts of the face scene?

"Well, here we are." The train station. How I bided my time there I don't remember but I do remember the sight of him waiting in a very long line and his return, what seemed like hours later to say what I thought was going to be goodbye. "Well, doesn't look like I'm going to North Africa." I can't remember what the hitch was. "Let's go back to the hotel, High Speed."

Yet another long walk in the hot Spanish sun? Why not? John Wayne shit.

✯✯✯✯✯

I FORGET which parade it was...Thanksgiving? St Patrick's? Santa Claus?...only that a light snow was falling, and that as I trudged indifferently from my late morning rounds back to my apartment, she, to the out-of-tune horns and drums, stopped me. "Hey, Dan! It's me."

So it was, the brunette last seen in a musty college doorway, diplomatically rebuffing me for impudently pressing my body against hers (in spite of my spotty high school record, I was able to attend Film Studies classes as an Adult Student).

"Oh sure." I was cooler than the air—I hoped. "Hi."

Some more chitchat—films, mostly—and then, the glimpse down at her feet. Beside her stylish boots, a child, thoroughly engrossed in the parade. Four? Five?

"I'll see you again some time," I offered fliply as the conversation petered out. "Yeah," she said, her voice charged with an anticipation that surprised me. "I'll definitely see you again." Oh, I realized: a single mom.

True to her word, this tiny brunette with the even tinier brunette did see me—in her miniscule walk-up, on a thin but welcome dinner-and-a-movie premise, in a yellow cotton dress that gave her a prim, old fashioned aura.

She had laid her finest porcelain inheritances out on her smallish dining room table—a hastily converted dining room I might add, badly hidden toys protruding from every cranny—and, to a scratchy recording of Terence Trent D'arby, served us both some quick-sale steak.

Almost all she spoke about was the scheduled after-dinner entertainment: a Top Ten of hers I had never seen, *The Thin Man*, with William Powell and Myrna Loy as husband and wife detective team Nick and Nora Charles, the witty, intelligent, and playful couple we were currently trying to imitate as we strived to achieve synchronicity.

More *Thin Man* talk as we cleared. Then, finally, after a quick check on her sleeping child, the film.

I had never seen somebody so into a movie. Yes, she had definitely shown enthusiasm during our college screenings, but nothing like this. Years later, taking my own daughter to the movies, my offspring's total involvement would take me back to that smallish apartment.

Yet suddenly, at the film's most involving moment, Nick Charles' revelation of the murderer, I felt the sudden, suggestive rubbing of a small, stockinged toe. Just a nudge; body language, I told myself, for "Isn't this a great movie?" or "Wow! This part is so exciting I can hardly stand it!" But the more information Nick imparted, the greater the rubbing. By the time he had carved his suspects down to a short list, the toe was demandingly tickling the back of my knee.

What was going on here? Was it possible I, or just plain sex, was suddenly usurping her hitherto implacable interest in the film?

Not wanting to appear clueless, I scooped her tiny form into my arms, *Gone with The Wind* style, and—Nick Charles be damned!—led her to the bedroom. Yes, like Nick, I had definitely read the clues. By the time Nora was congratulating her husband on a job well done, my hostess and I were halfway through a long roster of cosy cóntortions.

I awoke alone in a slice of sunlight, birds twittering, dishes clanging. I bounced out of bed, determined to cross to the kitchen, wrap my arms around her appreciatively and, a la Nick Charles, collect my congratulations from her on a job well done. What I had forgotten about was the possibility of a roadblock. It aimed its chubby, four-year-old face at me, point blank: "Did you sleep with my mommy last night?"

I froze as if I'd been put on pause. Then, with my best Grinch-to-Cindy-Lou-Who-smile, I came out with a faux-sweet, "Of course not. Your mommy and I watched a movie last night."

I had fooled her, but only, I knew, momentarily. I made a quick excuse about an early appointment, and, much to my hostess' disappointment, high tailed it out the door. You see, she had taught me a valuable lesson the night before: make your move before the detective figures it out.

✰✰✰✰✰

WHEN BASEBALL FILMS—*Bull Durham, Major League, Field of Dreams*—became the vogue, I toyed with writing one. I had no hook, no plot, no characters; just the central dynamic—a talented, egotistical star and a flirtatious, fiery female fan—and the slogan for the poster, a play on the then popular AIDS-prevention catchphrase: "No Gold Glove, No Love."

I would keep the idea in the outer recess of my mind, like a worn, yellowed outfielder's mitt hidden deep in a closet, occasionally taking it out and examining it.

The biggest prompt took place in a kitchen, in a stylish walk-up I had been invited to share with a newly married couple.

Their union suffered much criticism by our overly judgmental circle (largely due to their differences in age) but what I witnessed day after day was the loving glow of two people genuinely, giddily in love.

Was this in store for me, I would, in my too frequent episodes of self-pity, begin to wonder? While they'd be sharing a night out on the town, an evening cuddled on the couch, or jokes and jibes while performing mundane household tasks, I would be unceremoniously escorting my latest one-night stand to the door or finding the stocking of a departed lover I still pined for under my bed, heartache's calling card.

One night, with my landlords out cooing, I was part of a neighbourhood-rousing row. It was a wide-eyed blonde, with more integrity than I had guessed, berating me for not taking our relationship seriously enough. I began to realize, as she went on, that as she contested, the bodies had indeed piled up so high I had become incapable, no matter what caliber of lover I was presented with, of anything other than a romantic hit-and-run.

She continued, using words like "callous," "cowardly," and "selfish." They stung at first but by the third or fourth attack, I was back in that aforementioned closet, digging out that well-aged glove. I attempted to field everything she threw at me. No verbal equivalent of the errant throw, the hard bounce, or the little looper was going to get past me.

The odd one did, though, and so in the end, the dynamic I had been holding on to for years had finally become embellished: the story of a hero who could handle anything on the field but when it came to life, had great big holes in his game.

By the time she left, I was ready to start writing my baseball script.

Only one question, as I watched her blonde hair bob out of my life:

What price story?

✫✫✫✫✫

"A LOT of people lived in that house at the time," a renewed acquaintance recently reminded me. "I know," I said, "I married one."

The subject in question was wearing a blue bathrobe. It was ratty, I seem to remember, though today, many years later, I'm certain I was wrong; after all, I have lived with her mania for cleanliness now for almost half my life. I know I'm right about the other details, though: her tousled hair and tired eyes, for those too have become staples of my existence. Had I told her then, at that moment, while she was making herself soup after a long night on the town, that that particular physical combination gave her the look of a French movie star—a kind of Anglo Jeanne Moreau—I would have experienced my first flash of those oversized teeth, which, with a sudden toss of the head and a tensing of her muscly neck, was what you got whenever you made her laugh—a tradition that, I'm happy to report, continues.

Instead, I contented myself with remaining silent, awed by her presence while she stirred the soup, watching from the nearby table at which I sat with her roomies, friends I had recently made who were bringing me into their fold, the last echo of commune-style living. Talk of the shared conventions of their lives broke out—university, travel, parties—and I realized in a few simple lines that despite the striking face and the flash of perfectly formed leg that her bathrobe had offered, this woman's best feature was something that you could not, unless she spoke, discern: brains.

My intimidation, I was certain, would abate as I got to know her better. Maybe she would even return my admiration by becoming as aware of my unique charms as I had become of hers. Not a chance. Any such process with this person, I came to discover, took weeks, months, years. And so, the more I got to know her, the more distant I felt.

It was an alienation rooted in other factors, too: our ages—she had five years on me—our backgrounds—rich (her) versus poor (me, alas)—and our body types—athletic (her again!) versus thin (me again!). Still, I knew from our brief encounters that beneath the surface of all of that lay enough commonalities to sustain something: our love of high art, of popular culture, of involved discussion.

Our first date took place at—where else if you're going to go out with me?—the movies; Merchant-Ivory's first international success, *A Room with A View*.

As I waited for her in a long line at downtown's newest art house, The Phoenix (a block from which, unimaginably, we would be living together in four years), my mind began to reconsider my usual first date agenda. Given this woman's intelligence, maturity, and reluctance to go out with me (she had been seriously coerced), I knew I could not use moves left over from my adolescence. This was an occasion that called for the utmost decorum.

Good plan. Too bad she showed up wearing the shortest skirt imaginable and smelling of intoxicating French perfume.

To this day, I cannot tell you one scene—not one frame, in fact—of that Merchant-Ivory classic. The only masterpiece I saw that night was her, and that I can describe in minute detail.

We parted. A few get-togethers later, she took the gamble, informing me—with notable apprehension albeit—that she felt ready to attempt a relationship.

Years later, on an anniversary, the plan was to go out not to a movie but to dinner. Times were tough again (it happens all too often when you're in the arts) and that was all I could repay her with for what, all those years ago, she had chancily given me: the belief that some crazy how, we could grow as one.

You see: brains.

☆☆☆☆☆

HE WAS the greatest romantic singer of the twentieth century.

Small wonder my wife and I had our biggest fight to his music.

One rainy afternoon back when we were just dating, I entered the car she was driving and informed her that it was over. It wasn't of course—I was still madly intoxicated by her—but I was desperately looking for a specific reaction, namely, a "don't do this to me...I love you...I can't bear to be without you." .

In short, I was looking for her to violate her stalwart character in the most dramatic, inconceivable way possible.

This was something she had never done—not when her parents had brought her to the brink of vulnerability with the exposure of their long-suppressed relationship problems, nor when her drug-dependent brother had asked her to serve as his human shield, not when school or work tried to cripple her with epically unreasonable commitment.

So, if she did it for me, just me, then I would truly know that she loved me.

Surely Frank Sinatra, egging her on through the car stereo, would inspire her to action. Frank, half tough guy, half sentimentalist. He had overcome the fickleness of show business, had built palaces in the desert, had elected a president. He could do anything—even win me her.

"Okay," she replied indifferently. "It's over."

Two sounds usurped Frank to fill the sudden silence: the singular pounding of the rain against the windshield and the thunderous sinking of my heart to the depth of my innards. Where had Frank disappeared to? Why had he left me alone with the burden of coercion?

The tape, like our relationship, had ended unexpectedly.

Frank could sing like he did because he was no stranger to

heartache. He had company now, another fallen romantic made hard by reality.

✯✯✯✯✯

I WAS CONVINCED I was going to look like Cary Grant.

I would emerge out of that change room and every woman in the hotel—from the lowliest costume fitter's assistant to the blonde, haughty production supervisor—would gawk.

Never mind that I was a mere twenty-one, weighed less than the average order of bachelor's groceries, and hadn't the slightest notion of composure. Once I put on the tuxedo they had assigned me, the name would be Cary, not Danny.

I emerged from the change room, doing my best to negotiate the oversized plastic shoes I'd been issued. I brushed the curl that kept escaping the 1920's-style trim I had just undergone and tried on a killer smile. Despite the sincerity of their effort, it came out more like an apologetic snicker. It was nothing compared to the snicker I got from the girls, though. One of them even rolled her eyes.

"I see the party's started!" she commented to a co-worker. All thoughts of me even remotely resembling Cary Grant faded fast, like a Beverly Hills tan over a Canadian winter.

Nevertheless, after much fussing and adjusting, I was made to look reasonably acceptable—acceptable enough to be directed to the set, the grand ballroom of the Chateau Laurier, where the hundreds of others, each looking better than I in their vintage garb, were busily rehearsing everything from Old World dance moves to bits of incidental business.

The centre of this dressy storm was Christopher Plummer, who, alongside a happy, pasty newbie, was playing the lead in a TV bio about the Vanderbilts (the film, made for television, can still be seen late at night on the sorrier movie channels).

I joined the excited throng—movies, at that time, were rarely shot in Ottawa, particularly ones of that scope—and was immediately overcome by an overwhelming sense of...anonymity. Not seconds ago, I had allusions of taking the set by storm. Now, all I might manage was a possibility of precipitation...that is, until a mouthy A.D. wrapped a fat, hairy wrist around my licorice whip thin arm.

"You! Come with me!"

Before I knew it, there I was, busying myself at the buffet table to the immediate left of the two stars—in the scene, at that, where the characters first meet, a scene that couldn't possibly be excised from the narrative.

They would see me, all of them: my mother, my father, assorted friends. Already I could sense the jealousy in the room, eyes asking "How the hell did he score that?" Soon, whispers about the injustice of the underfed, inexperienced young dweeb being unfairly awarded primo screen time would surely break out.

The end of the day came, and, with the smell of gelatin-encased foodstuffs still fresh in my nostrils, I lined up breadline style for my fee: an American fifty-dollar bill. Exhausted, I went home.

A few months later, there it was, on television: *Little Gloria Happy at Last*, at last!

The ballroom scene, right off the top. The buffet table. Plummer approaches, makes contact with his co-star and....the camera goes into the tightest two shot ever framed. Further, it stays there! "I'm there!" I yell at my wife-in-the-making, pointing to the lamp just off the TV set. "I'm right friggin' there!"

Oh well, I sigh, as the story segues to the subsequent scene.

Maybe if I'd looked like Cary Grant.

✯✯✯✯✯

WE WOULD REWRITE THEIR DIALOGUE.

Frustrated that we could not belong to their world—that the best we could manage were pale imitations: local TV ads, instructional videos, bit parts in visiting productions—we would discount the paradise in which they operated by putting our own words into their mouths.

"Have a seat," a Hedy Lamarr or a Marie Windsor would offer an overweight character actor. "Great," we would have him say as he settled on the settee. "I'm sure I can find some old Chex Mix behind the cushions." Derisive laughter by all, then, just as quickly, silence, as we all prepared to ply our ventriloquism in the ensuing scene.

"My hand is crippled," lamented Cornel Wilde, as the maligned aerialist in the overblown *The Greatest Show on Earth*. "This is terrible," we added for him in faux French. "I'm a Frenchman. How will I talk?"

We never picked good films, of course—only the bad, the dated, the overrated. The ones that could best boost our collective self-esteem, best assuage our hurt, best deny our resentment over the chasm between Ottawa and Hollywood.

One of us would hit a streak—a series of teaching modules for some government department, a radio ad campaign, a summer theatre run—and suddenly, nobody felt like getting together anymore. No use eating Cheetos, drinking beer, and laughing at the incongruity of success.

But a long drought, more norm than deviation, and there we would all be, gathered once again in someone's living room, riffing off the screen and exploding with laughter.

Between films—at least two were shown at each gathering—there would be a lull while our sides recovered, followed by idle murmurs of "So, what are you doing these days?" or "Anybody heard from their agent lately?" (we had a choice of two). There'd be small talk about things that might be on the horizon or rumours of this or that production about to get going...then, inevitably, instructions to put on the next feature.

"Honey!" a helmeted gladiator would berate, through one of us, his wife. "I said 'Order aluminum siding—not aluminum sideburns!'"

And we would laugh ourselves into legitimacy.

✯✯✯✯✯

"Is THAT YOU?" a new acquaintance asks, walking into my office for the first time and noticing the large photo that hangs over my computer. "Oh...no. That's not you," he realizes.

The mistake is flattering. It reminds me of the only other time in my life something comparable occurred: walking out of the Expos' spring training facility, in a team jacket, carrying a bag from which a bat protruded (I had caught the game on my way to the airport from a Florida baseball camp). A near-sighted old lady, who had attended the Expos' drubbing of the Cards that day, came up to me and said, "You played so well this afternoon."

I've been out of the hero thing for a long time now—I've grown comfortable enough in my own skin not to want to wear anybody else's—but if there's a man I still identify with, it's him, the one who's softly smiling face looks down over me every day as I type, the God of Creativity to whom I write-bow.

I often reflect on the irony of *Citizen Kane* having been one of his favourite films and remember that scene in one of his films in which a childhood version of himself cleverly engineers a theft of its stills from a movie house. In much the same manner, I have had to steal images of him, Francois Truffaut, albeit anecdotal ones.

Like the shadowy reporter in *Kane*, I have made it a habit to seek out anyone who has known him. The count, so far, stands at three: a bohemian, a bookstore owner, and an actress.

The bohemian, a tall, sophisticated brunette who might list her occupation as hobnobber, had the most limited encounter: she spied him across her table at a Paris restaurant, where he was eating with one of his daughters.

More substantial is the tale collected from the bookstore owner, the sober-faced keeper of an LA. memorabilia shop Truffaut liked to visit whenever he found himself in Hollywood. "What was he like?" I eagerly asked him. "He could be accommodating but mostly he was very focused."

The actress: Teri Garr. Later, in various books, there'd be allegations about an affair with the sexually popular Truffaut. I didn't know that at the time—she was appearing in a film I had written—but did get one small insight from her: "The film I was working on with him, they had this extremely expensive champagne for the stars, and this much cheaper stuff for the crew. Francois was the only one to take note of this. He said, 'Non, non, non!' He made sure that everybody had the same champagne."

It's a crudely drawn character sketch I've managed to put together, showing an attentive parent, a polite but preoccupied public figure, and a vocal champion of the underdog; in short, a small affirmation of many of the qualities reflected in such films as *Small Change, Day for Night*, and for me, the life-changing *400 Blows*.

Like a dedicated pointillist, I'm still amassing dots—I've made a note to reconnect with a reporter acquaintance who I think once interviewed him—and hope to someday have bunched enough of them together to constitute a grand representation, one that reveals the man's Rosebud, the essence to which we can attribute his creativity.

I know mine: the squinty eyes, the sly smile, and the Napoleonic nose looking over me as I type.

✮✮✮✮✮

THEY WERE CLOSING, one at a time. They were taking up the crimson carpet, snipping the velvet rope, unhooking the thick, pleated curtains. Now, they were committing their most serious offense yet, at least in Ottawa: the removal of the balcony.

The Somerset was the last echo of the palaces of yore, where the Barbara Stanwycks, Gene Kellys, and Burt Lancasters had once flourished. Size that it was, it enjoyed a monopoly on the grandest fare, from *Star Wars* to *A Passage to India*.

Of late, though, it was more catacomb than pleasure dome. People, thanks to VCRs, were settling more and more for an experience well shy of spectacle. What fate, then, awaited it? A grocery store? An office complex? A concert venue?

One of its final breaths of life, ironically, was imbued with the theme of eradication: *Schindler's List*, Steven Spielberg's realist take on the atrocities of the Nazis and a lone voice, like the remaining minority of Somerset-goers, raging against the force of a purported progress.

Suffering his final breaths too was an impish young actor, the token gay personality of Ottawa's smallish theatrical community (as far as we knew) thanks, tragically, to a new and deeply unforgiving scourge known as AIDS.

Ravaged to a raisin-like countenance, his trademark energy evident only in his eyes now, he demanded, on one of the last days of his life, to be brought to the equally doomed Somerset, to see this film filled with debilitation and death. Sad but perfectly fitting.

Dutifully, a kindly member of our fraternity wrapped the actor's bony body in a blanket until he resembled another Spielbergian hero, the semi-disguised E.T. He cradled him in his arms like an oversized baby and brought him into the Somerset.

A few weeks later, the actor was dead, the first victim of this strange, unstoppable disease that I knew. Sometime after that, the Somerset too was gone and again, something once alive and special and perpetually welcome was lost.

For months after this twin killing, my mind played the final words of Italian director Luchino Visconti, the third casualty of that time: "I am not at all afraid to die," he said. "One must go see what is on the other side. It'll be like going to the movies."

☆☆☆☆☆

"THAT THING that you just told me," she countered, staring at me from across the table, "all of these men finding me attractive and coming on to me…it's not true."

Impossible. Impossibly impossible. After all, she was the prized possession of our social circle: green eyes, russet hair, mile-long legs.

"You're unhappy," she explained to me, her climactic conclusion of all that I had just confessed: my marriage, young as it was, already too demanding…the intimacy between my wife and I, becoming catch-as-catch-can…and that most trying of recent developments, fatherhood, for which I as proving hopelessly unprepared.

"What you're looking for," she explained, "is something… completely different."

Meaning what—her? Her with her addictions, her suggested promiscuity (denials to the contrary), her willingness to so easily break up a budding, if fragile, family?

What was there that might possibly rescue me, that might offer me remedy from my constant feelings of inadequacy, of immaturity, of unwantedness?

After all, what had we shared?

A night at my apartment after a film we'd been in together—my wife was out with the baby—where the much-ballyhooed "Central American snow" so common to her, so unknown to me, had been shared…*The Godfather 2* whizzing by, as a result, in what seemed like seconds…and, my senses barely senses at this point, a diplomatic peck on the cheek and an equally diplomatic "Next time."

Yes, I was full of questions. Yet it frustrated me that I could not succumb, that I could not enjoy a guilt-free transition to what now, weeks later, she was proposing with such frankness. It appealed to both the romantic and the rebel in me and titillated my almost defining instinct for self-destruction—perhaps the one thing she and I truly had in common. A few memorable moments together and then what? A joint dive into the abyss, I knew, the highlights all but memory in no time.

"...I can't," I answered, my voice a mix of regret, frustration, self-pity and could it be? - commitment, commitment to my predicament.

"I'm sorry," I added. And I was, particularly moments later, as I watched her slim, inviting form saunter away into the winter night.

I finished my coffee, sighed, and headed out for the apartment, the wife, the baby.

Say what you will about Michael Corleone, I reflected. He was no saint—but he was a good family man.

✯✯✯✯✯

ON THE SURFACE, Halloween sounds like every child's dream: for the price of simply donning a costume, and it doesn't have to be a particularly inventive one, one can get oodles of candy from both neighbours and strangers.

Come to think of it, I found myself pondering, it does seem too incredible to be true; no wonder my child, all of three, is staring up at me like I'm playing some foul, Wicked Witch-style trick on her. "Not going!", she announces, which I know is preschool speak for "I don't believe you!"

"Jessie, I'm telling you. It's true!" On and on I go, desperate to share this ritual with my daughter for the first time.

Finally, after many apprehensive squints of her perfectly round face, she concedes to wearing the little dress and cape that instantly convert her from a chubby blonde with disbelief on her face to Little Red Riding Hood.

I hold her high in my arms and proceed to our first house. All the while, I'm hoping that the mile-wide grin on my face will wipe away her last vestige of skepticism. It's not working. She still looks like a kicked pug.

I ring the doorbell, deposit her before the entrance, and, just as she turns to bolt back into my arms, the door flies open.

"She's addddoooorabbblllleeee!", gushes a house full of college girls, who immediately paint her face with kisses (dad is mighty envious of daughter), comment on her clothing, and load her up with more lollipops than adorned the set of *The Wizard of Oz*.

"Bye bye, sweetie!", they all wave, and with that, the door closes on our first Halloween encounter. Jessie sits, legs splayed, on the doorstep. There's the quick lick of a hastily selected lollipop, a cross-eyed look of love of sugar, and a cautious glare back up at me. "Dad," she starts quietly, "I LOVE THIS!!!"

You'd think that this would have bought dad all the credibility in the world; that from that magical transformation on, anything that I suggested would be accepted with uncontested enthusiasm.

But here I am again, pleading: "Come on, honey, it'll be fun!" and getting the same old squinty reaction.

Is my daughter, like my wife, going to be the kind of moviegoer classified as "temperate"? Is this ritual that has so defined my life something I am not destined to share with my own flesh and blood?

"Not going!" is the answer.

"Don't force this one on her," my wife implores, though she, uncharacteristically, is the one who had come home from a toy store the other day ranting and raving about how cute the characters in this latest Disney flick—something called *The Lion King*—are.

I work on Jess a few more weeks. I bring home picture books, plastic figurines, and other matters related to the film, slyly indoctrinating her into the culture until, I hope, she decides that she has to take that ultimate step, has to go see *The Lion King* with her father.

A few weeks later, on a Sunday afternoon in which our plans go completely awry, I re-state my original plea. "Come on, Jess, it'll be fun!" What do I get? "...okay, dad!"

Eureka!

Off we go, to the local multiplex. These are not the more intimate theatres I grew up in, they of the single-to-three screens, noiseless lobbies, and commercial-free previews. Nevertheless, they do share some traits with their ancestors: the greasy waft of freshly made popcorn, the growing buzz of the anonymous hordes, the pimply faced ushers in their ill-fitting uniforms.

As I, all smiles, purchase the last of our snacks in preparation of at long last passing the torch of movie-loving to my daughter, I am met by the stern visage of my not-so-long-ago happy wife. "Our daughter," she announces, "She's very upset!"

What can it be? What is it that is suddenly, unexpectedly threatening to sever this all-important bond yet to be tied?

The noise! In this age of the cash-grab multiplex, I had failed to account for the overwhelming nature of all of this aural stimulation.

The darkness? The darkness maybe, that's it I theorize, recalling my first experiences as a kindergartener, barely able to watch *Snow White* for the foreign, cavernous, claustrophobic feel of the theatre.

No. The snacks. They're not right. There's sugar and then there's sugar, and these are simply too removed from the crackers, apples, and slices of cheese that are the staples of her snack times.

What the hell is it?!

"He ripped this!!!" she informs me, brandishing her just torn ticket, her face red from crying as she aims an angry little index finger at a sorry looking usher.

"Now I can't go!"

"Relax, honey," I smile, "We can go."

✮✮✮✮✮

"WE'RE NOT USING it this weekend. If you'd like it, it's yours."

With that simple act of generosity, we announced to our pint-sized daughter that we were about to experience a family first: that all-Canadian ritual, a weekend at the cottage.

My wife and I entertained visions of barbecuing, swimming, reading novels in the sun. Our daughter, much to our surprise, was hedging her bets on encounters with bumbling dwarves, talking wildlife, perhaps even a dark-haired prince who would ride out of a clearing to bestow a kiss.

"Honey," we explained, "it's not like *Snow White*."

That film, the first I had ever seen, was also one of her first—albeit I saw it in a theatre, The Regent, and she, born in a more culturally diluted age, in our family playroom, with bears, balls, and crayons on the floor and cracker crumbs dancing from her chin.

"Aaawwww," she let out, disappointed. This was it, I realized, that first seminal separation from a world where all seemed possible, that first soul-crushing realization that you are not a citizen of a universe populated by anything remotely fantastic, enchantingly extreme, or beyond banality.

It's a tough lesson. I remember being highly disappointed that she had to learn it by way of such seemingly good news:

that our kinder, richer friends had seen it in their hearts to flip us the keys to a large, modern cottage on a private lake, on one of the sunniest weekends of the year.

"It'll still be fun," my wife and I insisted. "We'll swim, we'll hike, we'll eat outside..."

It was all to no avail. No family-created ritual, no act by mere mortals, could rise to the fun-filled conventions of those colourful, comic creatures she remained certain, up until our announcement a few seconds ago, were alive and well just a hundred miles from our home.

Nevertheless, we packed our dour faced little pumpkin into the car, squeezed her between enough bags for a month-long stay, and headed out for our retreat in the woods.

We pulled up, and as the wheels of our car grinded over the gravel, the cottage revealed itself to us in all of its Better Homes and Gardens glory.

"Look, Sweetie," we gushed. "Isn't that great?"

If she had a kindred spirit at that moment, it was Grumpy.

My wife and I entered, unpacked, then, slowly and with measured steps, our little princess followed. She scanned the room with an expression of sheer granite.

Finally, her eyes grew wide and bright, and her smile as broad as the lake outside the central room.

"Dad! Mom!!" she cried. "Look! Loook!"

Our eyes followed hers to...a broom. A simple, worn, nondescript kitchen broom.

"She was here!" our daughter deduced. "Snow White was here!"

As further evidence, she picked up the broom and recreated the famous dusting scene, in which the dwarves attempt to sneak a cloud of cough-inducing refuse under a carpet. "Ah ah ah," sweetly admonishes Snow White. "Not under the rug!"

"Oh my God, Honey!" my wife and I both marvelled. "We were wrong and you were right!"

Proof, after all, was proof.

✯✯✯✯✯

"DON'T YOU REMEMBER?

"You had bought this cereal when you went out to do groceries. I don't know what it was—some sugary thing we don't eat any more. You had told our daughter about the big prize you could win: 'Movies for Life.' All of a sudden, she started jumping up and down excitedly saying, 'Movies for life! Movies for life!' Then what did you do?

"You left!

"You went…somewhere! And there I was, stuck with this jumpy little four-year-old screaming, 'Movies for life! Movies for life!' Well guess what? I opened the box once you were gone and gee, what a surprise: no movies for life! Not even something saying Sorry, Try Again. And I was the one forced to explain to her how these stupid contests work.

"She was four! Try telling that to a movie crazy four-year-old! Now she's in absolute hysterics. Tears were streaming down her face. 'But dad said I could have movies for life!'

"I think she thought that if that wasn't in the box, this coupon or whatever the hell it was supposed to be, that she just couldn't ever go again—period. That you needed that coupon to keep going.

"And we had just taken her to her first movie, *The Lion King*. Remember how much she got off on it?

"…Is any of this starting to sound familiar to you, Dan?...No?...Hmm. She doesn't remember it either.

"That's probably because you've taken that kid to so many movies since, she probably remembers that she did win."

✯✯✯✯✯

INT - A TYPICAL SUBURBAN HOUSEHOLD. Dinner. Mom gives her daughter the umpteenth speech on the importance of eating salad. Dad, looking to endorse his wife's discourse, asks her to pass the dressing. With a condescending nod to their child, Mom wraps her fingers around my picture, and hands the bottle to her husband.

At least, that's how it could have been—for once upon a time, I came very close to being Paul Newman.

The film was *Mr. and Mrs. Bridge,* one of the quirkiest—and least successful—choices of property for a film ever made by the hit team of Merchant-Ivory. This dry, simple tale of an aging couple was slated to be shot, in part, in Ottawa.

Why come to a place with no studios, no rental houses, no development labs?

The answer: the odd bit of just-right scenery not to be found in overcrowded Toronto or in equally teeming Montreal—in this case, early post-war upper-class tranquility.

Two friends of mine, with whom I was appearing in a stage show, had secured bits in the film as ambulance drivers. Their instructions were to stake out all night in Rockliffe, Ottawa's tony suburb, and wait in the snow and ice until director James Ivory barked at them to do something. Halfway through the evening, he did: looking to get warm, they took refuge in an empty camper; Ivory told them to get the hell out of his trailer.

As all of this fun was going on, I received a panicky phone call at the nightclub where I was slated to perform (my comedy troupe, born of the ad agency I had once toiled for, was going great guns). My agent. Paul Newman's stand-in had gone missing. They desperately required a new Newman.

The idea struck me as capital A absurd. Me—Paul Newman? I was five ten, wore owlish glasses, and could only woo a woman after a month's worth of pleading and begging. "It's okay," my agent assured me. "It ends up you fit the costume."

You mean...Paul and I...me and Paul...Butch Cassidy and the

Can't-Dance Kid?

Of all the ways I could have possibly imagined he and I might be alike, that was definitely not one of them.

The agent went on: my job would be to stand in knee-deep snow, dressed in an overcoat like Paul's, until—yes—director James Ivory barked at me to do something.

"Um...sorry," I was finally forced to say. "Can't do it." My two colleagues had wrangled their absences from the show a long time ago. A last-minute replacement for yours truly would be more difficult to arrange.

"You know"—we're back in the suburban house now—"I was almost Paul Newman's stand-in," brags Dad, his daughter now watching him turn Paul's face upside down until a gooey green mixture spills out from the actor's head.

"You were?" she responds, eyes suddenly wide.

"I was. Quite frankly," adds Dad, addressing his wife, "I'm half tempted to tell the world that I was. After all, you know what they say: never let the facts get in the way of a good story."

"Daddy," says his daughter, sharing a sudden brainstorm, "I'm going to go to school tomorrow and I'm going to tell all my teachers that my dad was Paul Newman's stand-in!"

Suddenly, what had been no more than an effort to break the age-old dinner time parent-child salad debate was now a tension-filled lesson on the tricky art of imprinting morality on the young—complete with look of utter condemnation from my wife.

"Uh...," I countered wittily, "eat your salad, honey."

Paul and I might share the same height but not the same cool.

☆☆☆☆☆

I NEVER GOT IT.

Thousands did though, all around the world; some before my

time, some during.

The one my mind returns to surprisingly often lived just down the hall from me, in a boarding house. She had a complexion of chalk—moon-white and dry as a package of soap flakes—and for contrast, jet-black hair, oily and reflective, like the feathers on a raven. In short, she could have been drawn by Charles Addams, had his penchant been for the melancholy as well as the macabre.

She kept largely to herself—as most people who live in these kinds of arrangements do—and was known to me only by the occasionally forced greeting in the hall. It was Judy who was her real voice, at least to me; I spent many a night trying to read while she blared Judy's live rendition of *Over the Rainbow* over and over and over again, this through prolonged bouts of crying, draining herself of whatever speck of colour remained in that paper-white visage.

Whatever that woman's pain was, Judy was both the stimuli for it and her comfort from it. Makes sense I guess, as Judy's complicated journey from wide-eyed wunderkind to down-trodden dame is the journey, minus the sequins, of so many.

Hence when my daughter, a generally happy sort, suggested that for our semi-annual Daddy-Daughter Day, we settle in front of a veritable library of Judy Garland movies, I speculated about the true nature of my little one's current life. Did this sudden identification suggest an inner sadness I had failed to detect? A transition from the purity of childhood to the potential messiness of oncoming adult life?

We made snacks, monopolized the couch, and took in The Parade of the Judys: Judy in ruby red slippers...Judy pining for St Louis...Judy giving up the farm for the stage.

Afterwards, as is her custom after having watched a musical, my daughter danced the remainder of the day away, pretending, with every histrionic bone in her body that she was Judy, Judy in all her guises.

Her energetic cavorting smacked of such innocence, such youthful panache, such uncomplicated appreciation that I immediately chastised myself for having let Sigmund Freud intrude on Daddy-Daughter Day.

Call me an avowed innocent but I'd like to think that that's it, that that's the thing that, until my daughter's dancing, I had never seen—not the Judy of the white-faced lady at the boarding house. The Judy of my house.

☆☆☆☆☆

"HOW DOES IT END, SON?"

Always—from the kitchen, the bathroom, the hall. Then…

"Never mind. Don't tell me."

She couldn't bear it, whatever—sad, happy, in-between—it might be: the conclusive parting of the lovers, the punch line of all punch lines, the big, it-all-turned-out-okay-in-the-end reveal.

There would be rapt emotional involvement, then, toward the film's last twenty minutes, a look at her watch, followed not much later by a see-through excuse: the still full glass in need of refreshing, laundry that had been left unattended, sometimes a forgotten bit of ironing. Anything that would take place a safe distance away from the living room, where the portal into Hollywood, an aging black and white TV set, sat.

It was my job to tease, to begin to tell the tale of the final few minutes, until, of course, I would inevitably be interrupted. The trick was to give her just enough detail so that various possibilities could exist, so that there could be no fast and hard, so that the sad could function just as well as the happy and vice versa. In short, never to let the film end.

"The police called," was how my sister first explained it to me. "She used to call me every day. Then, she stopped calling. I tried calling her for three whole days. So, I called the cops."

The police, who had knocked on mom's door, then entered with force. She was there alright, face down in her couch.

Her insides, I was later informed, had become her outsides. She had locked herself in her home, safe from the world, with only as many bottles of inexpensive liquor as she could afford as companions. One by one she made them a part of her body chemistry, desperate to accelerate the verdict of her doctor: that she had but little time.

Deprived of my father, with whom she had reconciled after her failed second marriage, but who had died, too young, a few years later, her life had become a series of discounted romantic adventures, B-Movies you could say, instead of the splashy Technicolor variety. There were characters the likes of which you saw buzzing around Bogart, anonymous semi-comic goons, each less brainy and attractive than the one before—a long way down from dad, with his movie star looks which, when I was a kid and mom a young mother, used to make the teenage girls in the neighbourhood swoon.

She was buried with nary a friend in attendance and not much family. Both had been excised from her life. The only ones there were those who genuinely cared, who still felt a tangible connection: my sister and I, who had staked her to a modest service based on what little she had left as financial legacy.

It was a shocking, unexpected and underserved ending.

I'd like to think she found some ironing or washing to do and missed it.

☆☆☆☆☆

THERE IT WAS. My name.

Oh, I knew there was the off chance. After all, that particular library, the main branch of Canada's most bilingual city, is dutiful as can be about stocking Franco-Ontarian authors. As I had piggy backed on one—Robert Marinier, a well-respected

Ottawa-based playwright—I could be reasonably sure that the work on which we collaborated might end up there.

There. That exalted there—as in, the play section. As in, a few shelves away from that other exalted section. From *the* section. From the film section.

The section I have spent most of my life, ever since my first trip to that centrally located eyesore at the age of fourteen, poring over.

How many fingerprints have I worn off reverently running my digits along the collection's spines? How damaged are my lungs from lovingly inhaling its pulpy residue? How limited is my eyesight from scrutinizing the footnotes of each precious volume, never getting my fill, even after countless visits, of Orson Welles, Ingmar Bergman, Federico Fellini, or Jean Renoir?

It's a section I still frequent, even if it stopped being the one that I go to first long ago. These days, in fact, it's third, after the New Fiction display and the Have You Read? station. Still, I never fail to experience some echo of adolescent giddiness as I ride the escalator toward it.

Some last, unsnuffable spark goes off inside me, a remnant from those headier days when I veritably shook with the knowledge that the world's greatest filmmakers were awaiting, if only in paper form, my company.

That marvelously uninformed time before I had ingested every film considered a classic, and then everyone considered a sub classic, and then everyone considered a sub-sub classic. Before I could answer every trivia question, before I had what it took to write movies myself, and then to write about the movies in a manner such as this one.

I may only be combing that section for its few new acquisitions these days but I never fail to pull out an old favourite. Like the veteran director usually gracing that volume's cover, it cues me, the actor, into a sense memory.

Instantly, I am who I was and where I was when I first read

it: a park outside the adult high school in the city's Italian quarter, where I found respite from the burden of belatedly finishing my formal education in a thick biography of John Ford...the upper floor of a house across from a downtown high school, where I would sit up in bed with the woman who would become my wife and read her the memorably bitter bon mots of Pauline Kael...the worn couch of our first home, where I would point out a thick insert of publicity shots from MGM musicals to my Gene Kelly-crazy daughter.

No book bearing my name sits on those shelves yet (might this one someday?) And yet, it's a great comfort to me that, thanks to my collaboration with the aforementioned playwright, as part of the library's catalogue, I'll forever remain close to the film section.

I can't help but draw a parallel to my parents, with their long, on again-off again relationship, and their ultimate and fitting fate: buried in the same cemetery but not side by side; more appropriately, just a few feet away from one another.

✰✰✰✰✰

IN HIGH SCHOOL, where, in spite of her special needs, she was fully integrated, she could not keep up. She knew the moves well enough, she had been dancing ever since she could walk, and currently belonged to two reputable dance troupes—but the speed at which the other kids flip-flopped, flailed, and flung their lightning-fast limbs was but a blur to her.

She'd come home, rehearsal after rehearsal, not only with tired feet but with a broken heart. Given her limits, how was she going to fulfill her dream? How was she going to go to Hollywood, land of those musicals she so loved, and find acclaim as a dancer?

We consoled her, my wife and I, told her that her strengths laid in other genres of dance—but she would not be appeased.

Late one winter, fed up with Ottawa's unenduring cold, I suggested a sojourn south. My wife wanted no part of it. A trip, particularly a family trip, meant an agenda, and the daily routine of looking after our demanding daughter had taken its toll. "How 'bout you two go and I'll stay?" she joked. "Now that's my idea of a vacation!" And so, a holiday for two it became!

As for the location, where else would a movie-loving dad and his equally film-fixated offspring venture? To Lala land the Lalandes!

We toured Warner Brothers, where she astounded-annoyed fellow tourists with her irrepressible embellishment of the tour guide's patter...met a few of her idols, some flesh, some wax... and downed burritos and milkshakes at the hip Hollywood hangouts she had researched online.

Near the end of our stay, we cruised, as all visitors do, Hollywood's much-travelled Walk of Fame. At a designated point, the latest hip-hop hit, blaring from some strip mall, proved too infectious. Right then and there, without giving her father any notice, she went into the routines that in the context of high school, had deemed her a misfit.

Yet here, free from comparators, she shined like the L.A. sun. All shackles—her body type, her disability—were immediately danced off. Within minutes, I had lost sight of her. It was near impossible to keep her within my range of vision, as it had been seriously narrowed by a growing throng of appreciative fellow tourists.

They watched, cheered, filmed. They took out handfuls of money and implored me to offer the Dodgers cap I had recently purchased as a charity box. Eventually, the music stopped and a wild round of applause broke out. My daughter bowed, a beam of absolute triumph on her face.

After all, here she was, in Hollywood, an acclaimed dancer.

✰✰✰✰✰

This was it.

After how many films—thousands? Tens of thousands? Millions?

How many had I absorbed since that fateful afternoon when I was first taken to The Regent Theatre to see *Snow White*? This, the climactic transformation, though, was not the Wicked Queen's but mine: from watcher to participant, as, incredibly, but a few blocks away, a film crew was busily setting up lights and cameras, in anticipation of the hallowed Hollywood-born call of "Action!"

Within minutes—was this remotely possible? Was I still in bed, dreaming?—I would be joining them. I would enter an air-conditioned trailer, be fussed over for some script-dictated shirt and pant combo, help myself to free caffeine while sneaking peeks at some chatty make-up lady's cleavage, then, be ordered to the set.

Okay, this wasn't Hollywood, only my own backyard; this wasn't a major blockbuster, just an independent feature; and it wouldn't be in theatres, just try its luck on the festival circuit. Despite all that, though, no passerby, seeing the cameras, the lights, all of those busy, happy people devoted to a common, insular task—could deny that this was indeed that most bonified of things: a movie—a genuine, no doubt about it, perfectly respectable movie—and there I'd be, not just an extra or a stand-in or a bit player but one of the electrons of its nucleus.

I had told all my friends, from childhood forward, that someday, this absurdist miracle would absolutely, without question, come to be. I had informed my parents as well, dashing whatever working-class hopes each of them had that their son would end the generations-long tradition of struggle to find the biggest dream of all: middle class sustainability. And of course, I had told each of the girls I had tried so desperately to charm during my brief collegiate tenure.

Now, though, all of them might actually see that crazy dream of mine come true—at an art house somewhere or at least on some lazy afternoon on television. "Hey," they'd shout, "I know that guy!" And add, either internally or externally, "What do you know? He did it!"

Indeed, I had done it—thanks to a self-made producer-director (risen from the ranks of my advertising days) who doggedly showcased my writing and acting talents...thanks to bored, frivolous, and generous investors who went looking for a brand new kick...thanks to an ever-loving wife and daughter who enjoyed the monopoly of never once having looked at me funny for staking our lives on this chanciest of businesses.

I put my breakfast dishes in the dishwasher and took a deep breath. I glanced, for the umpteenth time, at the digital numbers on our microwave. In less than half hour, I would be the thing so many people once dreamed of and continue to dream about but that few ever realize—regardless of such distinct advantages as ability, tenacity, or, that most frustratingly elusive of things, good fortune.

"Well," I told my wife, trying hard not to grin self-congratulatorily, "I'm off to be a movie star." Gee, this might be, it suddenly flashed through my mind, my last act as a mere mortal. If this film exceeds all expectations, I continued musing, I might have just committed my final bow to mortality, poised to transmute, as the Bogarts and the Gables and the Davises before me had, into something larger-than-life.

I crossed to the front hall, put on my coat, and opened the front door. The streets that led to the set were flooded with blinding yellow sunshine—the kind of benediction that might have been concocted by Cecil B. DeMille.

"Dan," I heard a distant voice call out. I turned. Before me stood my wife, holding forth a smallish paper bag. "Don't forget your lunch!"

✩✩✩✩✩

ALL THAT STOOD between him and the beer he so desperately sought was a half wall and the kid behind it, hauling case after case.

"I said hi, kid."

"Hi," the kid finally returned, not bothering to look him in the eye.

"Nice cargo you're haulin'."

"Heavy," he commented.

With each lift, the veins in his under-developed arms popped, the same, dramatic way sets of eyes popped on the umbrella-holding passersby as they spotted Pat Morita, of *Karate Kid* fame, in, of all underused movie locations, Ottawa—and for some reason, on this wet Sunday morning, at the back entrance of some anonymous bar.

He was between takes—we were shooting an indie, one of five in which I was writer-co-star. He was desperate for the liquid courage that had been getting him, to the constant anxiety of our overwhelmed director, through his scenes.

"Well allow me to lighten your load...," he persuasively purred, depositing an American fifty-dollar bill against the ledge of the half door.

The kid, barely noticing, went on with his business, hauling case after sweat-inducing case.

"Whatsa matter, you blind? That's okay," he added, teasing him with the bill. "That fifty's been in my pocket so long I'm sure you can smell it."

It was a wit he had developed as a stand-up, then in sitcoms, before the *Karate Kid* had come along and made him a household name.

"I see it," the kid, preoccupied as ever, announced.

"...one beer. That's all I want: one beer."

"Can't," he grunted.

"Can't? Why not?"

"Sunday morning."

"Exactly. Who's gonna know?"

"My brother, Gino."

Pat was wet now, every part of him—save his throat.

"Well tell Gino that there was a little something in it for him too…"

Another fifty, atop the first.

"…still not interested, huh?"

"I told you before. You could put a million dollars there…"

"A million dollars? What's that American? 'Bout a hundred and fifty bucks?"

Another fifty.

When was Morita going to give up, I wondered, as the rain kept soaking both of us. My job had been to keep him in his trailer between takes, to ask him questions about his career, his personal life—anything to keep him away from the sauce.

"You seen *The Karate Kid*? I said you seen *The Karate Kid*?"

"Uh huh."

"You know Mr. Miyagi?"

"Uh huh."

"Well that's me. You wouldn't turn Mr. Miyagi down, would ya?"

The kid paused…turned. For the first time since this sad, surreal exchange began, he looked Pat Morita, Mr. Miyagi, straight in the eye. A long sigh came out of him… was he giving in? Morita grinned triumphantly.

"Mr. Miyagi," he began, "I know you trained the Karate Kid to be pretty good."

"Damn straight."

"But my brother Gino? He could kick that kid's ass!"

The kid turned his back on Morita. Morita turned his back on the kid. Through a parade of puddles, I led the former back to his trailer.

"I tested him hard," he commented. "He passed."

Mr. Miyagi had trained another one.

☆☆☆☆☆

HE WAS PLAYING ANOTHER ITALIAN, a precedent that had been set with his Broadway triumph in *The Rose Tattoo* and was going strong in big, commercial releases like *The Godfather Part 3*.

This time, here in Ottawa, he was playing Preston Street's own Arturo, the story-telling ring maker, in an overambitious indie written by yours truly.

The day before his first scene, he had invited me to join those meeting him in his hotel room. After a quick discussion about wardrobe, he gently insisted that I read with him—a rare offer for a writer. Afterwards, Eli—he forbade anyone to call him Mr. Wallach—informed me that my writing reminded him of someone else's: Anton Chekov's (!) and suggested that I re-read that famed Russian playwright's short fiction.

The next day, in a jewelry shop just off the air-conditioned trailer he chastised us for procuring for him, he proved unpretentious, hard-working, and extremely social. He waxed humourously with those both "above" and "below the line," as they say in the business, about such noted figures as Groucho Marx, John Huston, and Marilyn Monroe.

More than once, he mentioned that he was toying with collecting these reminiscences in a book, to be titled, *In My Anecdotage* (the man loved a good—okay, make it a bad—line).

There was something else he liked to collect: vintage timepieces. Between breaks, he would spend his time combing the antique shops in Old Ottawa South, inquiring in that famous avuncular rasp about watches and clocks from various periods.

A few days later, his scenes a wrap, he readied for his return to New York—but not before accommodating requests for photographs. Just before the shutter snapped on our mutual portrait, he cheekily placed his head upon my shoulder, puppy dog style.

Years on, as he neared one hundred (he would die a few months shy), I began to fashion the message I would send him:

"Happy Birthday, Eli. May your clock never stop ticking."

☆☆☆☆☆

SHE WOULD GET TOO EXCITED: elongate her broad neck until her nose near touched the screen...scrunch her face into deep expressions of interest, until it resembled a used grapefruit...turn various shades of red, each variety cued by a twist in the tale...turn to me, when a line or moment baffled her, with wide, empty eyes...and, strangest but most endearingly of all, flap her little hands excitedly through the air, usually during the climax, as if a baby bird taking flight.

After the movie, though—usually an old MGM musical or something animated—it was goodbye, Dr. Jekyll, hello Mrs. Hyde. The residual energy, a commodity Einstein maintained cannot be destroyed, had to go somewhere—and so it did: toward my wife and me.

My wife was usually slapped or punched, while I, whom she preferred, was doused with a glass of water or a cup of lukewarm (thank god!) tea. Every gesture came with strict instructions, in the loudest and most certain terms possible, beginning with the notorious F word.

And so movies, that ubiquitous cultural commodity that had so enriched her special needs-life, stopped being a convention of our collective one. They were replaced, out of strategic necessity, by more passive pastimes: reading, board games, long walks outdoors. Occasionally, she would pine for the acrobatic Gene Kelly, or for poor, lost Nemo—displays of emotion we would divert as quickly as possible.

Strokes—though only twenty-six, she had suffered two already, one before and one after the recently uncovered neurovascular condition that had necessitated brain surgery—

are notorious for bringing on behaviours of all kinds; anger was not entirely unexpected. But anger triggered by the movies, by a thing she so loved, was a post-stroke phenomenon that baffled even her most knowledgeable caregivers.

Slowly, though, I was determined to re-introduce them into our life—at least, our father-daughter life. Sunday mornings, while my wife slipped off to much-needed church, I would settle with our only on the well-worn backroom couch, our favourite, thinning blanket over our laps. There, one finger nervously glued to the Off button of our remote, I would bravely test her tolerance of Danny Kaye, Judy Garland, or Pinocchio.

The secret, I soon learned, was to watch no more than forty-five minutes per Sunday, then, to expend what that precious unit of time inspired through a long exploration of our neighbourhood.

It was half a movie, yes—but it was no longer half a life.

☆☆☆☆☆

THEY WOULD BE at the doors of the theatre long before they opened, like eager cinephiles anticipating the next installment of whichever franchise was au courant or those brave, theatrical souls who, in little more than a pair of fishnet stockings and a top hat, would line up on a chilly fall night to catch, yet again, *The Rocky Horror Picture Show*.

In their rusted state, it was hard to imagine that therein lay the stuff that, once fed through the Mayfair's compatibly archaic projection system, would delight a crowd of aging Boomers out to see the latest Judi Dench or a gaggle of goatee'd Millenials jazzed about a new John Woo.

Soon, though, I knew, I would no longer be walking past them on my daily sojourn to work. Film was undergoing yet another technical revolution; digital projection was on its way. Cans of film would be joining blacksmith's tools and Cathedral-style radios in the display windows of the area's ample antique shops.

Life, at least mine at that time, was becoming more and more about loss. My daughter was growing increasingly independent (a welcome change, mind you, given her challenges), my wife and I were now celebrating the big anniversaries, and, due to John Lennon's famous musical contention that "life's what happens when you're busy making other plans," I was going to the movies less and less.

I approached the tower in which I worked (after my stint in film, I had landed in television) still thinking about those eroding cans of film. What if the Mayfair, which had started a crowdfunding campaign to upgrade its prehistoric projection system, came up short? What then, it being the only theatre left that I occasionally attended?

Prone, by this time of life, to periodic bouts of reminiscing, my mind took me to a summer afternoon on Somerset Street. There, a film I wrote was being shot, starring the irrepressible Ernest Borgnine. Over a break, Bill Kinsman, owner of downtown's flagship video store, shows up with a shopping bag's worth of memorabilia, eager for Ernie to sign each item. Obligingly, he does, with characteristic bonhomie—until he is handed a still from *The Wild Bunch*. He stops, looks it over for a long time, fights a losing battle with a tear.

"Great guys," he sighs, over the famous shot of him and his departed co-stars as a four-man battle line. "Great, great guys."

He hands the photo back, then, disappears back into the building where we're shooting.

Sometime after that, Bill Kinsman died too; where all of that memorabilia he collected ended up, who knows?

Convinced, while lost in thought, that I have dropped one of my winter gloves, I turn to look behind me. My footsteps have been entirely covered by falling snow. There is no trace of my journey.

CURTAIN

He sat, small, balding, hunched as if addressing the dusty floorboards beneath his heavy, old fashioned shoes and not the fifteen or so semi-interested people that surrounded him.

In his sad eyes and half-hearted delivery, one felt his soul pining for the days of yore, that faded era when film, and those who puffed themselves up by pontificating about it, attracted wannabe intellectuals the way Johnny Weissmuller's ear-piercing sing-song once beckoned wildlife. Once upon a time, four decades or so ago (four? Really?) they filled this very auditorium, a small, forgotten room in the deepest bowels of the downtown library. Here they sat in charged, vocal anticipation, their incessant murmuring about this studio era director or that fashionable foreign filmmaker the aural trailer to whichever Japanese or Polish or Australian film would soon be rolling.

Afterward, a self-proclaimed authority figure would stroll on to the stage and give them, peppered with oblique adjectives, exactly what they had come for: a pseudo-intellectual analysis, cobbled together from best-selling books by the even more erudite. This would be followed by a spirited Q and A that was like watching Fairbanksian musketeers go at it with cross-references instead of crossed swords.

Now, though, here they were, the very last of them (myself included), most simply exercising a fit of nostalgia for a brief, brighter time when film societies were an intellectual sandbox and not, as it appeared inarguably now, a pine box, complete with corpse MC.

I left early, installing even more disappointment, I noted out of the corner of my eye, in our wormy ringmaster.

I walked home along Bank Street—gateway, once upon a time, to side streets where stood the Somerset, the Capitol Square, the still-standing but empty Place de Ville—past the facades of the video stores that had killed the aforementioned get-togethers and had dumbed down, to boot, the product that had ignited them. Now though, in this age of rampant downloads, they too were no more, converted to coffee shops, corner stores, adult toy emporiums.

That wasn't the only thing that was finished when it came to the movies. So too was my involvement with them, as, over years that had flown by too fast, the production company in which I had been a partner had not only reinvented itself, it had relocated.

I crossed the bridge to my home in Old Ottawa South. Once inside, I toyed with turning on the television to see which long unseen classic I might re-enjoy via one of the specialty channels. But I was not in the mood. A vibe had been established—a funereal one I felt had to be respected.

I went up to the master bedroom and looked out at the moon. In so doing, my malaise, mercifully, lifted. I had done it, the glow of that luminous orb reminded me. I had crossed a much bigger bridge than the one that had just brought me home, the span from movie-loving juvie to writer-actor in no less than five, if little seen, feature films. Just as miraculously, they were all made here, in Ottawa, the mid-sized city where I had repeatedly enjoyed this most alluring, most difficult of arts, where I had dreamed about them as relief from domestic, educational and romantic woes, and where I had plied my trade—writer-actor—until achieving competency, then success.

Just like when I attended my first movies then, here I was again, wide-eyed before a beacon of magic yellow light. Only this time...the image it was revealing was me.

THE MOVIE THEATRES WE LOVED

"DUUUUUDE," purred my irrepressibly enthusiastic editor, in her girlish cool. "You know what you need to complete this book? You need meditations on each of the movie theatres that you mention. Give us the facts, yes, but give us your spin too. Movies are such a personal experience, as you've proven—but the theatres themselves are too, am I right?"

Right as rain—the kind you might have dodged, back in the day, by slipping into The Somerset or The Rideau or The Place de Ville. Therein you'd find plush seats, snacks you rarely indulged in anywhere else (who ate Milk Duds at home?), and the company of strangers as giddy about what they were about to see as you were. Movie watching, back then, was both a personal and a communal experience, almost unlike any other. True, you can enjoy a simultaneously solitary and group experience in a museum, at a music festival, or even in your living room watching TV—but it isn't the same. Let the French, with their love of intellectualizing all aspects of cinema, come up with the answer as to why not. I simply want to speak for so many of us, in Ottawa and beyond, currently deprived of that much-loved recreational ritual thanks to the scourge of COVID-19: I miss it—or at least what's left of it, the last great age of moviegoing having occurred in the Seventies and Eighties (unless you count the rise of the suburban megaplexes. I don't.

OTHERWISE, this practicing nostalgist would have to have his license revoked).

So, let's rewind. Settle in, let the lights go dark, and enjoy these "shorts" on Ottawa movie theatres of the past...

THE NELSON

325 Rideau Street

The Nelson Theatre circa 1973. Note the Restricted sign below the marquee—the bane of my adolescence.

I DOUBT there was a better year for film than 1975. 1947, at least financially, was the biggie: all those soldiers back from the war, thirsty for much-missed pastimes. But in terms of "good screen," not "good green," not much of note was produced: *Odd Man Out, Miracle on 34th Street, Body and Soul.* The aesthetic crown belongs to 1939, whose output—*The Wizard of Oz, Gone with the Wind, Stagecoach,* and other blockbusters have been written about ad infinitum.

In 1975, though, those two all-important strains, the artistic and the economic, enjoyed a perfect fusion, like hot butter and popcorn. The "new American cinema" that had been rising from the ashes of the big studios (most of MGM, by that time, had been sold off to developers) broke through the mainstream for good—and a dense, discriminating demographic, soon to be labeled "The Baby Boomers," became the leading cultural crowd. They'd suffered the assassination of two Kennedys and Martin Luther King; had protested Vietnam and Nixon; had advocated for civil rights and gender equality; had investigated new ways of seeing through experiments with drugs and Eastern mysticism. Now, they wanted to see their energy, their issues, their vision on the screen. They wanted domestic film to go deeper, be grittier, take more narrative and technical chances, like the ground-breaking European ones they had discovered. The result was film after film made with a distinctly American integrity using European influenced cinematic technique.

Then, there were the critics. Hitherto, movie reviewing had been the "soft beat," assigned, more often than not, to any old reporter, who happily took the job as a welcome respite from chasing ambulances or soliciting quotes from politicians. Now, though, they were smart, lifelong film nuts who could riff on the latest releases with the literary panache of Tom Wolfe and the skew of Hunter S. Thompson. Not that the movement didn't have its populists—foremost, a fat guy and a skinny guy fronting a cute little show on PBS. But suddenly, movie reviewing had become as much an artform as the movies themselves, as much a pleasure to read as a good short story, and the hippest, coolest job anyone could have.

Like everybody else at that time, I, though all of thirteen, tried my hand at it, imitating make-or-break film reviewer Pauline Kael of The New Yorker (badly, of course; I'd use words like "kinaesthetic" without even knowing what they meant) in a series of foolscap notebooks I kept in my closet, the one with the back-light poster of the Marx Brothers on the door (most kids had Aerosmith or Kiss). Not that there was much that I could see. At that time, Ontario remained stickily true to its Protestant roots. Life ended at 8 p.m.—except for the movies, and those conformed to a strict code of admission. The single drop of a four-letter word, the mere suggestion of sex, a premise based on a cultural issue the world remained politically ambivalent about and if there was the slightest trace of acne on your puss, you'd be pointed in the direction of the latest Walt Disney production (*Taxi Driver* vs. *Herbie Goes to Monte Carlo*. Sigh!) Still, when I could pass for fourteen or over, I'd get to see a Nicholson, a Pacino, a Fonda (acting, too, had hit an incredible peak)—but certainly nothing foreign, which, mind, you, I probably wouldn't have understood, in spite of the subtitles, anyway.

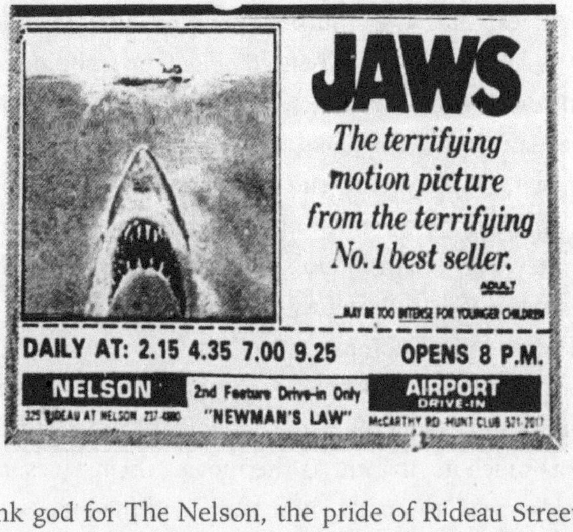

Thank god for The Nelson, the pride of Rideau Street, home of *Jaws*, which permitted me to experience the "new filmmaking," if one of its more commercial contributions, while unabashedly honouring my childlike sensibilities (director Steven Spielberg, who would make a habit of that particular man-child shtick, would eventually be begged by critics to get in touch with his "inner adult.")

Life began for The Nelson in that aforementioned boom year, 1947. Soon, it was competing with The Elgin and The Somerset as downtown Ottawa's flagship movie venue. If a picture was all the rage, you could find it at one of those three places. In my time alone—the Seventies and Eighties, considered by many American cinema's finest hours—I can remember trips to The Nelson to see *Earthquake* (in Sensurround no less, a short-lived gimmick where the theatre shook like it was strapped to the popcorn machine), *The Omen, Excalibur, Jaws* of course, and the cinematic climax of the decade, *Apocalypse Now* (where, when the white tiger pounced out of the Vietnamese jungle onto an unsuspecting Frederic Forrest, I pounced onto my best friend's lap!)

I can't tell you how many times I lined up in front of The Nelson to see *Jaws* that summer nor the extent of that film's effect on my generation—actually I can and do; it's in this book. I need add, though, that for years afterward, until the day the venerable Nelson, by then re-christened The Bytowne, unexpectedly closed (thanks, Covid!), I could not enter its confines without remembering, in pointillist detail, that particular experience.

The Nelson wasn't my favourite theatre but it was close. To its credit, while it endured a number of renovations over its history, it held fast against the removal of architectural grace notes suggesting its past: a semi-circular box office, where, one supposed, a gum-chewing ticket-taker with a voice like Eve Arden's issued you a ticket; its tile entryway, with its name proudly emblazoned in cursive type—deep brown on flecked beige—staring back up at you; its smallish lobby, whose on-off lighting mixed with that, during matinees, of the summer sun, trying to sneak in past the overzealous usher (rippppppp!).

And, of course, it had a balcony; big pictures only, please. When it was announced, in the late Eighties, that the city's leading art house, The Towne Cinema, would be moving there, I scratched my head like a lice victim. How in heaven were its staple of films—*The Rocky Horror Picture Show*, anything Fellini made, old Bogart pictures that played regularly on TV—going to fill so many seats? What Bruce White, its wily, dedicated owner knew, and I didn't, was that the film business was in serious flux.

VHS technology was relegating his cult-crazy catalogue to the rental shelves; already, he had plans to cherry-pick first-run independents and foreign fare, a formula by which he thrived for another thirty-plus years.

That, by the way, the rise of the video store (hands up if you remember Ottawa's first, Captain Video, on Bank Street? So new was the technology, you had to leave a $500 deposit to rent a VHS machine!) was what signified, cinematically at least, the end of the Seventies. Movies were no longer events; they were readily available commodities, kneejerk purchases like a chocolate bar or a Happy Meal. The Seventies then, with 1975 as its showpiece, was the last era when film was film.

Need more proof? Look at the Best Picture nominees. FYI I can not only recite them by heart, I can tell you at which theatres each one played: *One Flew Over The Cuckoo's Nest* (The Elgin; later, it moved to the Capitol Square); *Dog Day Afternoon* (The Place de Ville); *Nashville* (The Elgin); *Barry Lyndon* (The Capitol Square again) and *Jaws* (The Nelson).

The choice is not strictly sentimental.

THE REGENT THEATRE

NW Corner of Banks and Sparks

The Regent Theatre circa 1972. The marquee reads Lady and The Tramp —the same name of the double-act playing the strip club below it.

THERE ISN'T MUCH, at least on a personal level, I can impart about The Regent Theatre. In fact, until I began writing this book, I had never even heard of it.

Huh? How can that be, Dan, you're now asking; you've obviously been there. You mention it in the opening chapter!

I do. But childhood is a hazy thing. It's a jigsaw puzzle we can never quite assemble (even with the assistance, needed more often than not, of a sound psychiatrist). It remains, as it was in real-time, but bits and pieces, loose experiences devoid of proper narrative or geographical context. Vivid scenes are there but the where, the why, sometimes even the who are glaringly amiss. It's like a screenplay forever in development ("But what's the story, goddamnit?!") And so, while I distinctly remember attending *Snow White and The Seven Dwarfs*, and the familial shopping excursion that took place just before the screening, I had had no memory, till I decided to tackle this memoir, of the name of the theatre where that experience had taken place.

The Regent Theatre, it ends up, was wrapped around the

North-West corner of Bank and Sparks—a revelation found in Alain Miguelez's extensive *A Theatre Near You*, a coffee-table sized history of the movie theatres, from the single-screen glory days to the suburban cineplex movement, of Ottawa-Hull.

The Regent was there long before I crossed its threshold. Its history, in fact, spawns the bulk of 20th-century cinema: 1928 to 1972. The Regent was the theatre that, back in its infancy, brought that great industry novelty to Ottawa, talking pictures, proudly boasting the vaunted Movitone sound system.

While it played a variety of fare over the years, it was the exclusive home of the Walt Disney catalogue, both in first-run and as re-releases. Hence, my introduction to the movies: *Snow White*. True to its pedigree until its dying day, The Regent's final feature was one of the last theatrical go-rounds of *Lady and the Tramp*.

If social media sites are anything to go by, The Regent is often mistaken for its Sparks Street cousin, The Centre Theatre, later known as The Mall Theatre, which flourished over the same period. And while The Regent ended up with a strip club below it, The Centre's fall from Disneyeque grace was even greater: by the early 1970s, it was a porn house. Just as *The Seven Dwarfs* liked to sweep dirt under their rug (much to their prissy, porcelain-faced houseguest's sing-song dismay), Ottawa loved to do that too—at least when it came to its one-time concession to the pornography craze. Hitherto, that notorious genre had been the French's bent: the venerable Pussycat (what a name!) in Hull, whose black, rectangular ad was regularly buried in The Ottawa Citizen's daily movie section. But in time, this button-down town of ours indeed began to button down. The sexual revolution of the late Sixties brought with it a healthy appetite for the cinematically explicit—and so the Centre took it all off, as did The Mayfair and, occasionally, The Rideau (that is, if the zaftig bacchanalias of Russ Meyer count). Even the Britannia Drive-in would, once in a while, try its hand at it (pun not intended...I'm not fooling you, am I?) How many of our citizens, I wonder, led double lives at that time: Assistant Deputy Minister by day, raincoat-clad Onanist by night?

I was born too soon for that trend and frankly, I'm grateful. My love of good movies was such that even at that age, all I could do whenever I saw ads in the newspaper for everything from *Deep Throat* to *Debbie Does Dallas* was to internally cry, "What a senseless waste of a theatre! Think of what else they could be showing: all of those films that I'm always reading about, the ones that never show up on TV!" Spoken like a true film nerd. Besides, like most kids my age, if I wanted porn—the soft kind only, please. I was just discovering the stuff; don't frighten me off of it!—I could watch that Saturday night staple, *Bleu Nuit*, on the French TV station, which ran the artsy-fartsy *Emmanuelle* canon ad infinitum (all that foggy cinematography. It was like watching people tease each other on a bad day in Newfoundland!)

Plus, I had my imagination, my own "cinema." I could have my own cast, picking out any girl or woman (I liked them a tad older) that I wanted—a Breck Shampoo ad-worthy drugstore cashier, a bookworm on a bus, my middle school Religion teacher (don't go there!)—and go as slow or as fast, sexually, as fitted my hormonal change du jour.

What was it that Truman Capote said about sex? That it wasn't the act of it per se that was the best part but the "cinema" of it, its fictionalization, either when you were recasting the act as it was actually happening or whether you were enjoying it without a partner.

A notion that for a few, forgotten years, had been at the philosophical centre of The Centre Theatre.

THE ELGIN THEATRE

216 Elgin Street

The Elgin, the first multi-screen theatre in North America.

THE THEATRE IN OTTAWA, for years, was The Elgin (ten points if you can remember which street it was on). But how many of you remember The Little Elgin, the original name of its second screen? And how many of you know that that particular addition made The Elgin the first multi-screen theatre in all of North America?

I became cognizant of this little-known fact when I was working at CPAC, the Ottawa-based political and public affairs TV channel. You're right: it was the unlikeliest place in the world for me to be working, save for the fact that I was in charge of making their commercials and I had a background in advertising. When you're born and raised in Ottawa, you develop one of two attitudes towards politics: you either embrace them wholly and become yet another political animal or eschew them entirely, convincing yourself that you're fated for an alternate destiny. As an artsy-in-the-making, I, of course, fell proudly into the latter category. Nevertheless, there I was, trolling for any ad-worthy statement of Stephen Harper's (talk about a needle in a haystack!) when I was seconded to subtitle a series of patriotic interstitials that we aired called *Canada's Heritage Minutes*. You've seen them: fast-as-lightning dramatic recreations of great moments in Canadian history, like the Parisian beaver hat fad or the Feng shuing of the Diefenbunker. One of them was the story of The Elgin Theatre and how its mustachioed manager had put the "plex" in "cineplex."

He was only trying to give the world more of that magical experience, the sensorial smother that is the movies—after all, he had done it to accommodate *The Bridge on the River Kwai*—but ended up, inadvertently, diminishing it. Soon, there'd be theatres boasting three, five, twenty-five venues, each no more than a box and a screen. Only in civil service-happy Ottawa, with its countless cubicle farms, could such an idea have taken hold!

The big theatre, though, which opened in 1937, was the real deal—and remained so till, ironically, the cineplex movement forced it to close in 1994, an ignominious demise met with mile-long petitions. The citizens of Ottawa knew that the disappearance of The Elgin was not only the death of one of the best places in the city to see a commercial film, it marked the end of Ottawa's downtown movie scene. There was the newly established World Exchange Plaza but that too was a cineplex.

For years, major movie houses were a symbol of a thriving downtown. A city without one on its main street was, regardless of size or population, classified a hick town. And now Ottawa, which was growing into an interesting mid-size city with a population nearing a million, a handful of professional sports teams, and a festival and culinary scene rivaling those of the metropolises by which it was squeezed (Montreal, Toronto) was, with this one concession to the changing winds of commerce, in serious regress.

The Elgin in the single-screen days, 1945. Note the jutting marquee, eventually outlawed.

The demise of those theatres have left a hole in the city's

heart that's never really been filled. After all, what can replace the excitement of lining up outside (yes, it being but two screens, you had to line up, sometimes for hours) to catch the promise of silent film-worthy pratfalls in The *Return of the Pink Panther*? Of having the option, back in 1980, of seeing either *The Elephant Man* or *Raging Bull*, knowing that the last time the place hosted two films in black and white was probably before you were born? Of waiting again, this time inside, behind the velvet rope separating a giddy mob from a waiting-to-be-filled theatre, and making friends, just to pass the time, with the off-tune whistler in front of you or the preening divorcee behind you, knowing full well that the friendship, like those struck on airline flights, would last but the length of the movie?

Oft times, you'd emerge so high on what you'd seen you'd cruise Elgin Street for whatever else the place had to offer, you and your companion verbally re-piecing key scenes together or co-nitpicking its violations of your shared aesthetic over smoked meat sandwiches, plates of hummus, or scoops of ice cream

The Elgin, then, offered more than one kind of illusion: foremost, the movies, but too the conviction that Ottawa was a bona fide city.

THE RIDEAU THEATRE

160 Rideau Street

Rideau St., back when its only drug dealers were mustachioed pharmacists.

In spite of being a lifelong (more or less) resident of the city, there are some distinctly Ottawa things I've never understood: Bridgehead coffee, Alanis, The Rideau Theatre.

The Rideau suffered, at least over my time, a serious crisis of identity. History suggests that perhaps 'twas ever thus. To wit: it opened as The Princess Theatre back in 1915, a mom-and-pop outfit bringing Douglas Fairbanks to the Byward Market. 20th Century Theatres (not yet wed to Fox) took over in 1931, renaming it The Rideau. Till it closed in 1982, the place was renovated constantly—an architectural revolving door, reflecting the accelerated turnover of its cinematic agenda.

Allow me to further support this argument, Your Honour, by submitting an ad hoc list of the films I saw there over the time I was a semi-regular, a period spawning, approximately, 1973-1982:

A Barbra Streisand double bill: *What's Up, Doc?* and *For Pete's Sake*. Once upon a time, The Rideau probably showed real screwball comedy, though the stuffy, socially-conscious Fox Studio wasn't known for producing much of it. Years on, the smallish Rideau was showing homages to it, in part to appease widespread mid-1970s' nostalgia for Hollywood's dissipated heyday (remember the *That's Entertainment* compilations?) Neither of these, *Doc* nor *Pete*, with quirky Babs going to great, goofy lengths for her WASPy boy toy, were in their original run, being, respectively, two and one years of age. Periodically, then, The Rideau would serve as the last, pre-television gasp for such films, boosting their final theatrical prospect by packaging them as a two-for-one deal.

Walt Disney's *The Aristocats*—Disney films were a staple of the Rideau. Wiley Walt made it a policy to re-distribute his pictures every seven years, convinced that by then, a whole new generation of kiddies would have grown to the age of admission, a hunch by which both he and The Rideau prospered. How nervous Ottawa's parents must have been, though, taking their kids to the wrong end of Rideau Street, transitioning, at that time, from a quaint commercial hub to the drug-dealing street party that it is today—not to mention the theatre's proximity to the Byward Market, then still owing to its boisterous, bucolic roots. Perhaps that was why by the late Seventies, releases like *The Rescuers* were playing a little farther up the street, at the much more respectable Nelson.

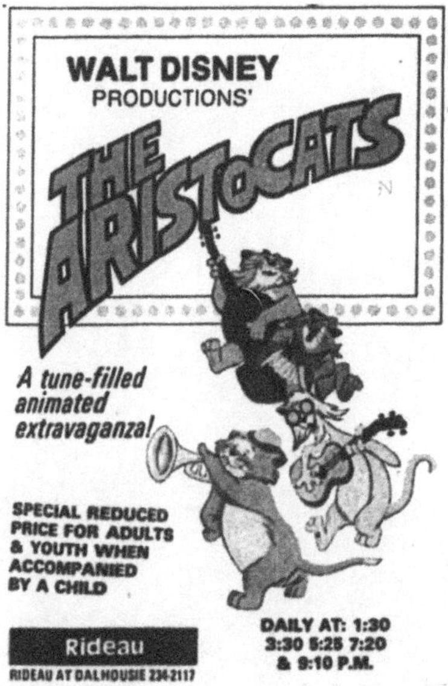

Russ Meyer's *Super Vixens*—See? I told you. When not flaunting Disney, The Rideau, at that time, was busy promoting another fantastical imagination: Russ Meyer's (sleazeball or satirist—you decide!) whose busty, lusty heroines were, as the Mount Rushmore-sized mammaries on the film's low-cut poster girl were deemed, "too much for one movie." This was the one concession over the long course of my movie-going life, FYI, to anything remotely blue. But as a devout leg man, I have to ask myself: what was I thinking?

The Rideau, then, was an anything-goes type of place, the landfill of Ottawa's movie theatres. You couldn't enter the place, unless you were going upstairs to shoot pool or play video games, without thinking that you were answering the W.C. Fieldsian call of a carnival barker, knowing full well that you'd walk away feeling, yes, entertained but cheated too.

THE PHOENIX (AND RIALTO) THEATRE

413 Bank Street

The Phoenix that rose from the ashes of The Rialto.

I NEVER FIGURED out why The Phoenix Theatre's life span was so short (nor Marty Feldman's for that matter, till I discovered he smoked five packs a day). Maybe Phoenixes just don't live long, except in legend. In no time, they're relegated to the ashes from which they've sprung, though this one didn't immolate, it was razed to make way for an office complex yet to be built.

No doubt the place was so named because it rose from the dirt, specifically, the kind coating the aisles of the Rialto a.k.a. the notorious "rathole."

The Rialto wasn't a movie theatre—it was a place for downtown's downtrodden to bide time, sleep off benders of Aqua Velva, dodge the nip of February, or enjoy the kind of sex not yet sanctioned by polite society.

The notorious Rialto a.k.a. "the rathole." There was more horror in the aisles than on the screen.

Management knew it, too; they'd play any ol' thing all-day-everyday, for but a pittance. Give me your tired, your poor, your huddled masses...anybody but a real moviegoer.

Film nerds to the rescue!

In the early Eighties, a group of Carleton University Film Studies students took the place over. They cleaned it up (brave souls!), installed a new kind of candy counter (serving baked goods and tea. What was this: Murray's in the Lord Elgin?), and showed, almost exclusively, foreign films. The city already had an art house, the popular Towne Cinema, but that was away from the core, in a neighbourhood not yet gentrified (though, yes, better than The Phoenix's when it was The Rialto). Now, downtown had a genuine alternative to commercial cinema, places where you could see Truffaut, Kurosawa, and the frilly folly of Merchant-Ivory. Like TV's then-popular *The Jeffersons*, The Rialto had moved on up.

Therein, perhaps, lies the secret behind its too-short life. The North American appreciation of foreign film, at its height when The Phoenix opened, petered out over the remainder of the decade. Tell today's *Star Wars-Matrix-Lord of the Rings*-raised kids that once upon a time, almost forty percent of Ottawa's movie theatres played intellectually challenging films in another language, be it Italian, French, Swedish, or even Polish, and you'll get the same look Princess Leia gives Han Solo when she first suspects he has designs on her.

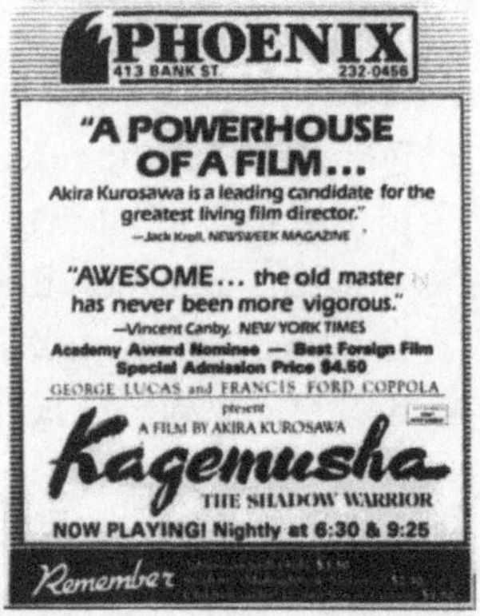

BUT EVEN IN LESS-THAN-COSMOPOLITAN OTTAWA, foreign films were everywhere, not just The Phoenix: the aforementioned university, where the witty head of the Film Studies department, Peter Harcourt, held court in the St. Patrick's Building; on newly minted TVO, where Elwy Yost struggled to explain them to us—and himself; the local PBS affiliate, which made a late-night staple of the vaunted Janus film collection (replayed Sunday mornings; you could have Rice Krispies with Roberto Rossellini!)

Then, there were the film societies, run out of the downtown library on Metcalfe Street, the Library and Archives building on Wellington, and other crannies, where groups, like today's ubiquitous book clubs, would get together to watch a bad print of an old Antonioni or an obscure Godard before taking it apart as if it were as important as Trudeau's latest skirmish with Levesque.

The movement forced everyone to access their inner egghead. A lot of bluffing went on (you can imagine!) as well as shamefaced revelations of one's middlebrow character. Plus, you'd be occasionally subject to the ocular delight of having to discern white subtitles against shots of wintertime Sweden (thanks, Ingmar. I'll have Lens Crafters forward you the bill!).

When the whole movement, The Phoenix included, died out, the majority rejoiced. No more having to think while watching movies! Bring on *Indiana Jones, Police Academy,* and *Revenge of the Nerds*! Still, some of us, whose love for the form ran so deep there was no deconstructing it enough, were left with souls bearing what now stands on the sight of the long-flown Phoenix: a great big hole.

THE SOMERSET THEATRE

386 Somerset Street West

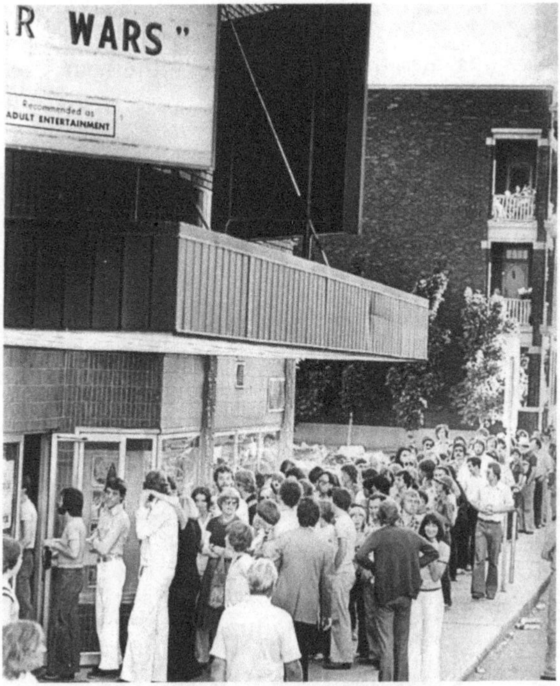

A long time ago, at a theatre far, far way…well, unless you took the #5 from Elmvale Acres.

"SPECTACLE" is the word that comes to mind whenever I remember The Somerset, my most cherished of all of Ottawa's long-gone movie theatres. Check out this sample size of what played over my prime moviegoing years: *The Three Musketeers, The Towering Inferno, Midway, Airport '77, Star Wars, Gandhi, Annie, A Passage to India, Schindler's List*....No venue in the city, though the dodgy corner of Bank and Somerset hardly suggested it, was better equipped for large-scale class, though The Nelson occasionally fit the bill (playing the *Indiana Jones* franchise, for example). After all, The Somerset had the most seats (730), the widest screen, and—best of all—that mile-wide balcony. Yes, I know: The Nelson had one too but somehow, it wasn't the same. The point is if a movie was all the buzz, you'd find it at The Somerset—and if not a blockbuster, then at least something so popular, you'd be turned away anywhere else, like the summer of 1978, when its ushers broke the hearts of many a collegiate yahoo by announcing that the next showing of *Animal House* was completely sold out.

It was the only theatre in Ottawa during my era—the utilitarian Seventies, when movie theatres began to be located in malls and office complexes (still magic to me, though)—with a tangible lineage to the palaces of yore, largely thanks to its aforementioned size and balcony (upon opening in 1937, it was advertised as "A beautiful new amusement place, located in the heart of the city."). True, The Mayfair harkened back to that gilded age the most, as much of its original rococo décor remained (peeling as it was—and that bathroom! It wasn't just vintage, it was prehistoric!) but tragically, it spent most of my formative years as a purveyor of pornography.

Entering The Somerset's expansive lobby, then, making your way into its equally spacious confines to vie for an elevated perspective, you experienced a bit of what your parents and grandparents did, back when movies, before they were homogenized by everything from TV to VHS tapes to DVD to streaming—were an event, life's only visually-based alternative to the staid nature of reality. It's what allowed them, for a few, much-needed hours, to forget the tribulations of the Depression, the daily horror of World War Two, the white-collar pressure of the Fifties.

Life at The Somerset was big, bigger than yours could ever be. It didn't exist, like other theatres, to reflect or question reality. It was there to exaggerate it. Dangerous deserts were crossed, polarized populations clashed, airplanes and boats were torn asunder. You went to be overwhelmed, immersed, dwarfed. When you walked out, whether during the day or at night, you felt like you had just enjoyed the privilege of visiting another planet.

The effect was exacerbated by the fact that, at that time, Ottawa was minuscule: about 350,000 people. Allan Fotheringham, the popular columnist, had labeled it a "company town"; instead of mining, it was politics it centered around, but that, according to him, was the only difference. There was more to the place than that, of course, but it could definitely be stultifying—hence, The Somerset, an essential service.

The crowd comes back for The Empire Strikes Back.

The Somerset, until it closed in 2000, was our Radio City Music Hall, minus the Rockettes—though there was always a leggy beauty or two in the summertime line-up snaking all the way down to the periphery of Dundonald Park. If I'm making more out of the place than reality afforded, then perfect—for that's exactly what the Somerset did.

THE ELMDALE

1196 Wellington Street

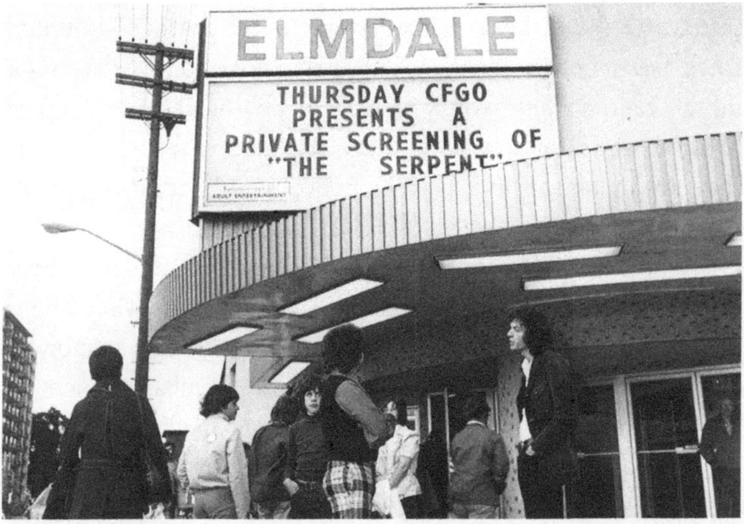

The Elmdale Theatre. Today, it's a church. Same crowd, I wonder?

ASIDE FROM THIS ONE, you won't find a mention of The Elmdale in this book. Why not?

For one, it wasn't a theatre I attended on any significant basis. I've lived in many different parts of the city in my time but few made The Elmdale an excursion of convenience. How well I remember my initial visit: my sister and I, one extremely snowy evening, had collectively decided that this foul kind of weather should definitely keep the masses away from the mega-hit du jour, the one so popular you couldn't get a ticket on bended knee: *Kramer vs. Kramer* (the only divorce in history, astute critic David Thomson's pointed out, where money is never even brought up!) And so, to Gloucester, then just transitioning from farmland to suburb, we ventured; Lawrence had an easier, and faster, time negotiating Arabia.

Was it worth it? No. The snow, the bus after bus after bus (remember paper transfers, in a choice of pink, blue or white?), and then, the final indignity, the theatre. Its lobbies—there was a lower and an upper—were promising enough (there were settees even) but the screening room! All the charm of an unfinished basement in Overbrook. Worse, those sorry excuses for murals on the walls: wonky stencils of Charlie Chaplin, Marilyn Monroe, and Brando's Godfather, tar-black on off-orange. Had the person responsible been a police sketch artist, criminals would have walked Westboro forever.

Westboro. Maybe that had been the problem. Today, it's the hippest 'hood in the 'Wa. But too many of us forget what a bona fide miracle that is, right up there with Lourdes and microwavable bacon. For years, it was a veritable embarrassment, a ghetto, really, of flea-ridden furniture stores, food inspector-free eateries, and Hell's Angels byways. It's only redeeming feature was the Parkdale Market, and even that had a kids' park where parents would repeatedly find used needles in the sand. Perhaps, then, The Elmdale was just going along with the crowd—though the fare it showed, like *Kramer*, suggested greater aspirations.

The Elmdale Theatre, back in the days of the Wild, Wild Westboro.

I know this hatchet job of mine breaks, decidedly, with the otherwise elegiac tenor of this memoir—but it's impossible to paint The Elmdale in the same poetic-nostalgic hue as Ottawa's other movie theatres, in spite of a respectable pedigree going back to 1947 (it closed in 1994). Though it may have since become a church, I still say it was beyond redemption!

THE CAPITOL SQUARE CINEMA

230 Queen Street

The Capitol Square Cinemas, where I would sneak from theatre to theatre. Defunct for years, the ushers are still looking for me.

IT'S HARD—NAY, impossible—to believe that the three-screen Capitol Square Theatre, the very model of Seventies maudlin modernity, was once one of the most prestigious movie houses in all of North America.

The Capitol, it was called (it became square, literally, later). "That was a beautiful theatre," I remember my father, a regular in the 1950s, telling me, going on to describe its lush lobby, marble staircase, box seats, and sea-wide balcony. By the time I got there, 230 Queen Street was a creaky escalator, a utilitarian concession stand, and rows of overhanging lights shaded by psychedelic dunce caps.

An acorn, then, from a mighty oak. Get this: when the Capitol officially opened in 1920, a train arrived at Ottawa's Union Station from New York City, carrying not only movie theatre mogul Marcus Loew but more than a dozen of the day's top stars. They were taken to City Hall and Parliament, then, paraded through the city, where throngs of celebrity-mongering movie fans came out to see them. Finally, the whole starry entourage was brought to the sold-out inaugural performance: a quartet of vaudeville acts followed by the latest D.W. Griffith production.

It's almost on par with the magical day I spent there over the Christmas holidays of 1977, where, dodging the preoccupied ushers (in their canary yellow polyester uniforms), I sneakily saw three hit films for a single admission, hahahaha: *Oh God!, The Goodbye Girl, and Annie Hall.*

While the place was a far cry from what it used to be—not only did it fill its 2,500 seats by showing movies, it hosted name acts over the years from Nat King Cole to Jimi Hendrix—throughout the Seventies and Eighties, the Capitol Square was a key member of Ottawa's downtown theatre circuit, along with The Elgin, The Nelson, The Rideau, and that other theatre put up in the Seventies, The Place de Ville. Life, for movie nerds of that era, revolved almost exclusively around that circuit; it was a sub-city, our second neighbourhood, our second life. Further, they were in very close proximity of each other (a business practice in motion today among the coffee chains). You could spend a day, providing you had the money, like a pinball at Frank'n'Fries (the Bank Street pool and burger joint, remember?) bouncing from one theatre to the other from 1 p.m., when the first shows started, to 9 p.m., the last.

Ah yes—the showtimes. They were standard then: 1, 3, 5, 7, and 9 p.m. You went after lunch, before dinner, or after dinner. You snacked on modestly sized popcorn and sipped from a cup of Coke a small child wouldn't drown in if it fell into it by accident. And somehow, the theatres survived, even though the split between the studios and the exhibitors was as one-sided back then as it is today, with the bulk of the ticket take going to the moviemakers. Later, in an act of rebellion, theatre chains would build on what Ottawa's Elgin did, when it added The Little Elgin.

They'd play the volume game, constructing theatres featuring countless numbers of screens. They'd up the sizes, and the prices, of their snacks. They'd make deals with fast food outlets and set them up in their lobbies. They'd desecrate the entrances with noisy, money-grubbing video games, air hockey tables, and those perpetually frustrating claw machines.

The three-screen Capitol Square, then, previewed what was yet to come. Back in the day, we didn't know that. Only that three heads (or two if you counted The Elgin or The Place de Ville) were more novel than one.

THE BRITANNIA AND AUTO-SKY DRIVE-INS

Britannia: 3090 Carling Ave / Auto-Sky: Corner of Fisher Ave and Baseline Road

Ottawa's first drive-in. The papers had to explain how it worked ("In the middle of the movie, you lie on top of each other in the back seat…").

"THINK ABOUT DRIVE-INS…" Jim Mackie, one of Ottawa's leading professional gurus back when the high-tech industry was usurping the civil service as the city's top employer, once advised. Jim—who, along with his wife Debbie, privately underwrote the five independent feature films I was privileged to have been a part of—was upholding the long gone drive-in as a golden example of the successful marriage between disparate ideas: automobiles and movies. By hybridizing things in this manner, Jim concluded, great, original ideas could be spawned.

Jim wasn't the first to experience such a flash. The inaugural instance (note: this is a much-debated history) belongs to an auto parts salesman travelling through California in the 1920s. Spying a rock face reminding him of a movie screen, he got the notion to project a film on it. Cars would stop to watch it, he theorized, at which point he'd have a captive audience for his auto parts. His next discovery, the big one, came after he'd essayed it: that people could care less about his camshafts and dipsticks but that they loved watching a movie in their car. Just like that, the drive-in theatre was created.

Six of them, starting in 1948, sprung up across Ottawa, led by the Britannia, at 3090 Carling Avenue. The concept was so new, the local papers had to explain how it worked. The first film shown was the Marx Brothers' *A Night in Casablanca* (not their best). But soon, as the Forties made way for the Fifties, teenagers took over.

It was actor-director Richard Attenborough, in his autobiography, who pointed out that until the Fifties, there was no such thing as a teenager. Adolescence was simply an awkward waiting room for adulthood. After the war, though, came the sexually pent-up ex-soldiers; in no time, myriad numbers of children sprung up. They'd grow to be the most affluent society of youth to that time—so much so that everybody would want a piece of them: television, the recording industry, advertising, and, of course, the movies.

Sure, The Britannia played *Ben-Hur* but it also played B-movies aimed at luring the teeny-

boppers, its cigar-chomping producers quick-buck capitalists fully cognizant that, in those sanitized times, a car was about the only place a guy and gal could exercise hormonal urges. Cue *The Creature From the Black Lagoon,* whose aim was to make angora-clad cuties jump into the lascivious laps of their duck-tailed Saturday night paramours.

The locals must have loved it. This, after all, was Ottawa in the Fifties—"the dullest place on earth" Christopher Plummer, who fronted productions at the time at the Ottawa Little Theatre, remembered—where the edicts of the church, whether you were English or French, ruled the behavioural roost. When Elvis was booked at the Auditorium (now the Argyle Street YMCA), my mother, all of sixteen at the time, remembers the nuns who instructed her prematurely damning anyone entertaining buying a ticket to the flames of hell (scared, mom caught the Everly Brothers instead, likely figuring that would just warrant limbo).

Along came, mercifully, the sexual revolution. Still, the drive-in stayed true to its roots as an adolescent drop-in centre. Many a zit-faced high-schooler, in his first car, would roar up on a Friday or Saturday night throughout the Sixties and Seventies, regardless of what was playing. It helped that the price was right, downright cut-rate compared to the sit-down theatres. The drive-ins would play this up, regularly staging "pack the car" nights (and when they didn't, you'd sneak your friends in under seats or in the trunk), a promotional gimmick which also appeased low-income families, who usually smuggled in homemade snacks.

The food, too, was cheap, though legendary for all the wrong reasons. Hot dogs cooked by lightbulb (always an oily red-green) and burger patties that would make coasters strong enough to endure a busy Irish pub. They sold a lot of it, though, particularly in the Seventies when Cheech and Chong began to make movies, creating periodic exoduses of hungry hippies from cloudy Dusters and funky-smelling Pacers who had been imitating their onscreen heroes.

The other thing that made it special was its seasonal longevity: drive-in life lasted, each year, but a summer. After that, management would put up a cheeky goodbye on its sky-high marquee (personal fave: "Closed for the season. Reason? Freezin'!"). The drive-in, then, became synonymous with things like summer romances, public swimming pools, and affordable cherries.

My favourite drive-in experience is recorded in this book, when the Auto-Sky Drive-in debuted *Star Wars*, an under-advertised sci-fi film I had a bitch of a time talking my family into attending. Looking back on it now, I realize just how unique that experience was—after all, *Star Wars* was an unknown commodity for but one night. The next evening, after the reviews came out, it officially launched its forty-year-and-counting history as an international cultural touchpoint.

Ottawa's drive-in screens went down, tragically, like Transformers-sized dominoes, back in the mid-Nineties. Why should we be exempt from a North America-wide trend? VHS-DVD culture killed it, just as it killed, albeit more slowly, a lot of the sit-down theatres. It hardly helped that the car was becoming an environmental Darth Vader. Every now and again though, I read an article somewhere about the drive-in's proposed resurgence.

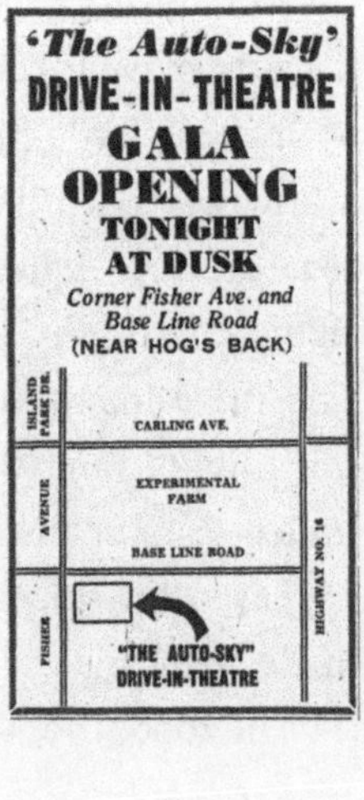

I hope it happens and I hope it doesn't. I'd love to see, say, the next *Planet of the Apes* installment en plein air but I'm not sure my back can take intermission-time sex in our boxy Fiat.

THE ST. LAURENT THEATRE

1200 St. Laurent Blvd

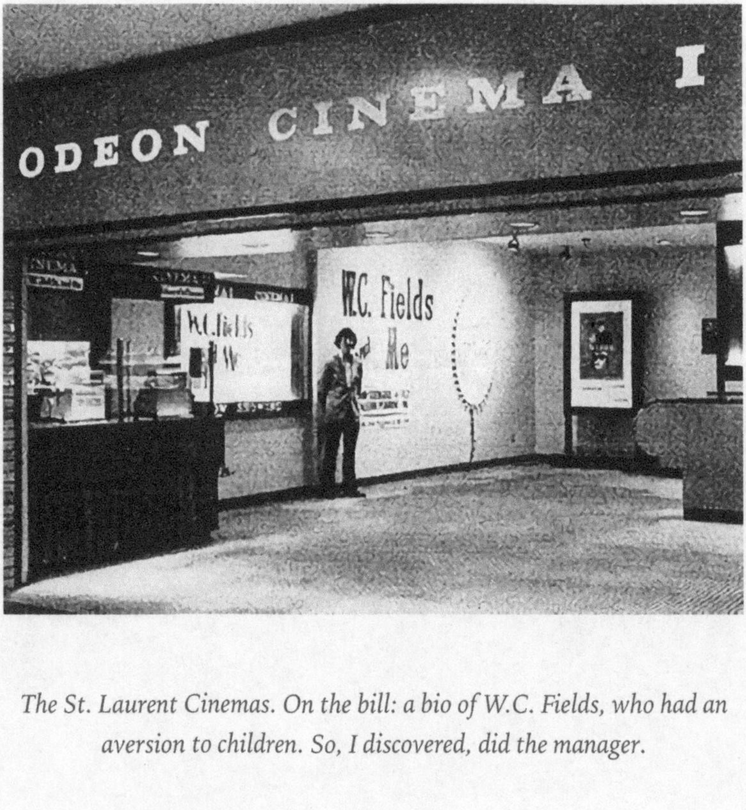

The St. Laurent Cinemas. On the bill: a bio of W.C. Fields, who had an aversion to children. So, I discovered, did the manager.

With the onset of its centennial year, Canada set out on a new, modern agenda. As the Nation's Capital, Ottawa was in for its fair share of this geographic and cultural renaissance—hence that godawful train station on Tremblay Road (in its defense, it boasted the city's first video game: Pong, of course). Part of the plan, too, though, was the establishment of the city's first mall-based theatre, within the confines of the St. Laurent Shopping Centre. When it came to the movies, the message was clear: single screens, rococo marquees, and lush lobbies were out; multi-screens (well, two), flat-panel signage, and long-haired teenage ushers, almost always in flirty conversations with the pony-tailed concession gals, were in.

Up until that time, there'd been neighbourhood theatres, like the smallish Rexy in then working-class Hintonburg. But this was the first suburban model, bringing movies to Overbrook, the St. Laurent area, and Gloucester, the latter an area just then transitioning from agricultural properties to prefab housing (even as late as the tail end of the Seventies, residents of its garden homes could wake up on any given weekday morning to the site of an errant rooster parading their front lawn, a refugee from a neighbouring farm, cueing them to rev up their cars for the long ride in to Tunney's Pasture).

If you've read the bulk of this memoir, you know that as an adolescent, I split my time between my on again-off again parents. Mom's, the respectable place, was located on Stonehenge Crescent, a community now as forked as a bolt of Olympian lightning. Our local theatre, then, was the St. Laurent, even if it was a good five miles away. Nevertheless, it was a walking marathon I would volunteer for on a regular basis (anything in order to get my fix), particularly as weekend busses to the 'burbs, at that time, functioned at the speed of Viking galleons (further, on Sundays, all of the itineraries and bus numbers would change, a notorious, short-lived system OC Transpo called "Orange routes.")

Still, it was almost always worth the journey. First, the much-needed exercise—as a sports-averse artsy (save for baseball), I faked every ailment I could think of it to get out of gym class ("I can't do the shotput, sir; my leprosy. What if my hand travels with the ball?"). Then, all that time with my movie-fuelled imagination. I'd replay cherished scenes from past and present favourites, fashion lists of actors' and directors' credits a la not-yet-created IMDB (a mental pastime to which I still subscribe, when I'm going through an extensive dental procedure, for instance, or whenever my wife goes into her long spiel about my sorry dishwasher-loading skills) and craft my first original screen stories. And then, the mall, one of but a handful in the city. I'd cruise the shops a bit, shoplift the odd film-themed book from W.H. Smith's, then, turn left into the crook leading to the theatre, home of *The Phantom of the Paradise, Tommy* (the frizzy-haired stoner in front of me, grown impatient over the coming attractions, actually took out a lighter and set his sneakers on fire), *The Buddy Holly Story* or *The Jerk*.

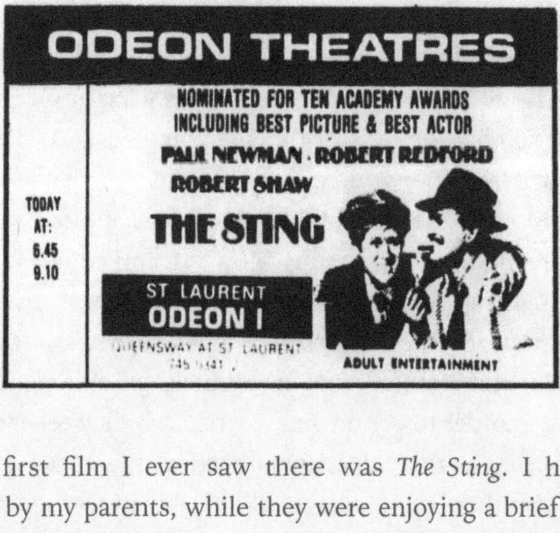

The first film I ever saw there was *The Sting*. I had been brought by my parents, while they were enjoying a brief reunion suggesting a second try at marriage (it didn't take, though they did recouple in their final years). It was the first film that made me conscious of all of the different components of a production, not just the writing, acting, and directing: the graphics, the costumes (those high-crown fedoras!), the music, the editing...

The other cinema was showing another big hit, *The Last Detail*—but there was no way I was going to be taken, on our next excursion, to that one (even if Mom and Dad could manage to get me admitted). The poster alone affirmed that I'd have to wait until the marquee, a heaven-high affair looking down over the mall's eastern parking lot, changed: a steely-eyed Jack Nicholson, in Popeye-esque sailor suit, summating the premise thusly: "No *#@!!* Navy's going to give some poor *#@!!* kid eight years in the *#@!!* brig without me taking him out for the time of his *#@!!* life." I was familiar with *#@!!* from Mad Magazine, which I faithfully collected (mostly for its film parodies, whose artwork I could copy rather well). And while I knew that these random collections of symbols represented swear words, I had no idea which ones—how mild, how strong. Later, when I would witness the argument my parents would stage that would definitively negate all possibilities of that first romantic reunion, I desperately wished I could replace each heated exchange with Nicholsonian hieroglyphics.

I had no idea at that time that for the succeeding years, before I grew old enough to venture downtown on my own, The St Laurent would be my go-to theatre. So comfy would I grow with its modest confines I would go on to suggest to dates that we venture there instead of downtown to see whichever film was all the buzz. In time, this became a litmus test: if they agreed, even reluctantly, it was a sign of genuine romantic interest; if they told me that the annoyingly long bus ride wasn't worth it, I knew that a cursory post-film kiss, in front of The Elgin or The Rideau or The Nelson, was all that I was going to procure.

My favourite St. Laurent-based memory involves a frizzy-haired flautist I once dated. I would wait for her outside the house in which she was having a lesson, the sonorous sound of her flowery flute serenading me from an upstairs window. Then, after a stroll through the woody-leafy Glebe, we'd hop bus after bus after bus till we made it all the way to The St. Laurent. By the time we got there, her first time at that location, the look on her face suggested that this skinny, movie-loving guy she had taken a chance on had taken her, barefoot, to Katmandu. This had better be worth it, her tense, hollow smile politely veneered. Roll film. Within seconds, there we were, one of two hundred or so astonished gawkers marvelling over the blinking spaceships invigoratingly bleating at us in *Close Encounters of the Third Kind*. That film not only earned me a kiss, it swayed her to gamble on me several more times—courtesies with which I was all too flip. Maybe it was the legacy of Mom and Dad, getting in the way.

PLACE DE VILLE CINEMA

300 Sparks Street

The Place de Ville cinemas. Talk about well-dressed ushers.

THE NAME: Place de Ville. If you didn't know any better, wouldn't you assume it was a tree-lined boulevard in central Paris, where mustachioed flaneurs treat their poodles to cups of café crème while they ogle Catherine Deneuve lookalikes? (FYI for more of this Franco-fied misconception of Ottawa, check out the 1952 film *The Happy Time*. While it's based on the coming-of-age memoir of a Byward Market resident, Hollywood had clearly never heard of Ottawa: citizens stroll the streets in Maurice Chevalier wear, spouting oodles of "Ooooh la la"s).

We, citizens of Ottawa, all know the truth: that it's a black and steel office complex—government offices on top, shops and food court on the bottom—on Albert Street, between Kent and Lyon, about as interesting as the monolith from *2001: A Space Odyssey* without the subtext. Over the course of my time, however, it's provided the odd, uncharacteristic excitement: first, a surprise visit by the Harlem Globetrotters, then at the height of their fame, strolling its grounds before their night's engagement at the Civic Centre, in hats the size of spaceships and ivory-coloured fur coats as long as *Ivan The Terrible Parts One and Two*, much to the unsuspecting delight of my fourteen-year-old friends and me. Next, the movie theatre, a unique "piggy-back" affair: twin theatres, one atop the other, like mating frogs. Further, they were separated by an hour-long escalator ride (or so it seemed) past a mural of twinkling lights, simulating the office décor at NASA.

Both theatres, one seven hundred-plus seats, its little brother four hundred, proudly exhibited first-run fare—though occasionally, one of them, due to some industry blip, would lose its standing, settling for a triple-bill of movies everybody had already seen (*Bananas, Up In Smoke,* and *Airplane!*, for instance) while the other, no doubt preening (it's hard to tell with inanimate things), would be proudly packing them in with the latest blockbuster.

Once, in 1976, they went mano a mano, each showing the same movie: Dino De Laurentiis' feminist take on *King Kong*. Management, of course, was anticipating the kinds of crowds they would have had to turn away had they relegated the film to a single venue.

The most exciting original motion picture event of all time.
2nd WEEK!
Dino De Laurentiis presents a John Guillermin Film
"King Kong"
WARNING: Some scenes may be frightening — Theatres Branch, Ontario
FEATURES DAILY AT:
CINEMA 1 AT 12.20 2.35 4.55 7.20 9.45 P.M.
CINEMA 2 AT 12.00 2.15 4.35 7.00 9.25 P.M.
Place de Ville 1 AT BOTH Place de Ville 2
QUEEN ST. 235-9546 QUEEN ST. 235-9546

It was a gamble, I seem to have read afterward, that, like poor, deluded Kong himself, ended in personal heartbreak and public embarrassment.

Perhaps, like that poster's tragically ironic image of Kong trying to ward airplanes off of the World Trade Centre, it was a haunting harbinger. For indeed, The Place de Ville would become a bona fide industry humiliation, of the everlasting variety. Andrew King, in *Ottawa Rewind: A Book of Curios and Mysteries,* calls the place "Ottawa's forgotten movie theatre." Forgotten because, though long closed, it's still there, in all its Seventies glory, seats and all. Visions of Miss Haversham's cobweb-strewn parlour in David Lean's *Great Expectations*—Theatre Number One—and Nora Desmond's cavernous Hollywood mansion in *Sunset Boulevard*—Theatre Number Two. "Anybody got use for a small stack of used movie theatres?" its landlords have repeatedly asked. But in this age Netflix and Disney Plus, no takers.

The last time I attended was with my daughter, then just coming of movie-going age (she has since become, like her father, a devout convert). The film wasn't worthy of its nosebleed-inducing escalator ride: an animated semi-atrocity featuring the voice talent of Macaulay Culkin, *The Pagemaster.* Leaving to enjoy cheeseburgers in the window of the newly erected McDonald's across the way, I became conscious that I had just ventured to that theatre for what was probably the final time (the cat had been liberated from the bag re its impending closure). A veritable montage of flagship scenes from the countless films that I had caught there—*Blazing Saddles, Nine to Five, Purple Rain, Batman, Glengarry Glen Ross*—rolled like a celluloid tsunami through the beachhead of my mind.

My eyes then fell to my daughter, who, I realized, with the closing of yet another downtown theatre (by 1996, they were dropping like flies), would grow into a "cineplex baby," likely going on to romanticize, as she grew to adulthood, the ear-splitting lobbies, coin-hungry claw machines, and KFC thrift boxes offered by the suburban multiplexes.

To each generation its magical memories.

THE TOWNE/BYTOWNE CINEMA AND MAYFAIR THEATRE

325 Rideau Street / 1074 Bank Street

Bye-bye, Bytowne!

ART HOUSES.

The Nation's Capital, a city once defined by the joke "What's the difference between Ottawa and yogurt? Yogurt has culture," boasted, remarkably, two of them.

The first was the Towne, later recrowned the Bytowne, at 5 Beechwood Avenue, gateway to what is now New Edinburgh. Back in the day, however—the theatre opened in 1968, as The Linden—there was nothing "new" about it. This was a rough-'n'-tumble neck of the woods; an Anglo Vanier. So, yes, the rent was cheap but that was all the poor, puny Towne had going for it. After all, its primary audience, university students, was miles away. It was a long trek from Carleton, even Ottawa U, to *The Rocky Horror Picture Show*, particularly in fishnet stockings on a February night.

It survived seven decades, two identities, and the ravages of Sensurround.

Still, the place made a go of it, thanks to the enterprising programming of Paul Gratton (who later stocked the Bravo TV Channel) and Bruce White, the face of both locations (the Towne-Bytowne took over The Nelson in 1989). Largely, Gratton-White offered a mix of classic and cult—plus, of course, those endless midnight showings of *Rocky Horror*, making it the only theatre with a concession staff that worked a graveyard shift. That was the standard art house practice in those days and Gratton-White made certain that we, small as we were, got more than our fair share.

Over the course of the Eighties, however, film, even the alternative variety, suffered mass homogenization. Even *Rocky Horror* you could pick up at your neighbourhood Blockbuster.

But what should have been a death knell sounded like sweet music to Bruce White.

White picked up The Nelson and, by switching to a program of foreign and indie premieres, cherrypicked from international film festivals, its cultured downtown audience: aging Boomers moving back to the core. Let the big chains live and die (mostly die) by the CGI-happy spectacle; the Bytowne would exhibit industry marginalia and thus sail a steady ship (hence, perhaps, the portrait of the 19th-century sea captain on one of the walls leading to the balcony, a dead ringer for the hirsute White).

But nothing, with the exception of *Star Wars* it seems, goes on forever. White, now white, was looking to retire—his first hunt for investors since he had purchased The Nelson. What came along instead was Covid-19, warding off prospective takers. Roll, too soon, credits.

32 wonderful years indeed.

The Mayfair, the Bytowne's brother in cinematic arms, is, gratefully, still standing. Has been, in fact, since 1932. It's been a first-run house, a porn palace, a rep-grind house, and now... uh...all of the above. Another proud ambassador of all things artsy, foreign, campy, and everything in between, local film-maker Lee Demarbre is in charge (what is it with hairy guys fronting movie theatres?)

The venerable Mayfair, the room for The Room.

Operating a no-frills single screen theatre in this day and age is like entering a Monster Truck show with a unicycle. But Demarbre, to his hardworking credit, makes a go of it. It doesn't hurt that unlike the Towne-Bytowne, the Mayfair benefits from a number of advantages. First, the building. It was declared, thanks to a push by Demarbre and company, a heritage building, resulting in reasonable rent.

Second, Carleton University, as well as an older audience as savvy as The Bytowne's had been, is but a stone's throw away. Third, they're damn supportive: when a make-or-break projection upgrade was required, the good citizens of Old Ottawa South floated Demarbre. And you can bet that with the sucker-punch closing of The Bytowne, these audiences—nay, the whole city—will keep The Mayfair even closer to its heart…er, art.

The Covid Horror Picture Show.

BEST AND WORST

I HAVE EXTREMELY fond memories of my first trip to Europe, in my time, a leading post-college rite of passage. The only thing that disconcerted me was this small sacrilege that they—the Spanish, the Brits, even the movie-crazy French—plain-facedly permitted in their theatres: the playing of TV commercials before the feature. Ha! I laughed to myself. Like that other tradition I couldn't wrap my head around, bottled water, I remember assuring myself *THAT'LL NEVER COME TO NORTH AMERICA*!

In my humble defense, when that money-grubbing practice did come to Canada, in Ottawa at least, people protested voluminously, booing and hawing from their seats and flooding the editorial pages of The Ottawa Citizen (there might have even been a few boycotts). The theatres, in-kind, respectfully apologized, then admitted that that ignominious practice was here to stay.

In time, another form of advertising, plugs for upcoming films disguised as trivia questions, joined the pre-film fray. Rejoice, readers! I'm not here to pick your pockets. Rather, I'm out to introduce a more respectable practice in the same spirit of those time-biding mind puzzles. Here are questions you, as a long-time Ottawa moviegoer of a certain age range, can ask yourself, each rooted in your personal experiences at the circuit of cinemas that is the centre of this book. Feel free to take or leave my own responses, predicated as they are on my eclectic personal aesthetic...

WHAT WAS THE BEST MOVIE YOU SAW AT EACH THEATRE?

The Elgin - ***Raging Bull*** (1980). Scorsese's masochistic masterpiece. Plus, unlike Rocky, Jake didn't go on to embarrass himself by trying to settle the Cold War through post-fight press conferences.

The Nelson - ***Apocalypse Now*** (1979)—with apologies, of course, to *Jaws* (1975). It was highly anticipated—the most talked-about film since *Cleopatra* (1963)—and didn't disappoint. That said, when, in the VHS era, I recommended it for a communal movie night, it lost to a John Ritter vehicle called *Hero At Large*. Moral: be as selective about friends as you are about movies!

The Somerset - ***Lawrence of Arabia*** (1989 restoration). I had seen it countless times on television, each time wondering what it must have looked like on the big screen—then, finally, my chance! I was so familiar with it I could point out each "new" scene. Dan Lalande: helpful guide or public nuisance—you decide.

The Rideau - ***Handle with Care a.k.a. Citizens' Band*** (1977) - It was supposed to be not much more than a low-budget attempt to cash in on the CB radio craze (remember *Convoy*, the song, the movie?) but a witty unknown was behind the wheel: Jonathan Demme. Small film, big laughs.

The Capitol Square - ***Monty Python and the Holy Grail*** (1975). I give it five out of five "Ni's!

Place de Ville - ***Blazing Saddles*** (1974). Call me what you will but it gets my nod for the famous fart scene alone. Why wasn't it in then trendy Sensurround?

The Towne / Bytowne Cinema – ***Last Tango in Paris*** (1973). "Due to a shipping error," I remember the handwritten sign on the doors of the Towne Cinema announcing that fateful summer night in 1981, "tonight's film is unavailable. Instead, we will be playing 1973's *The Last Tango in Paris.*" Grrrrrr! I've come all this way to see that Japanese documentary on sushi etiquette, I griped. Oh well…this won't be as good but…HOLY CRAP!!!

The Mayfair – ***Das Boot*** (1982). Wolfgang Petersen's claustrophobic classic. I still thank my lucky stars that American TV didn't appropriate it, take out the German fatalism, and call it *Das Love Boot*.

The Elmdale – ***True Stories*** (1986). An early date with my wife-to-be. This hip tapestry was so engaging that for the first time together in a theatre, my eyes were actually on the movie instead of her legs.

The St. Laurent – ***The Sting*** (1973). This boyish ode to chicanery culture, released at the time of Watergate, was a bona fide crowd-pleaser. Not a lot of it plays today, though. It's a lot of wink-wink amounting to very little—like my sex life 1973-1983.

The Phoenix – ***A Private Function*** (1984). As British comedies go, it sure beat *Carry On Girls!* (see the worst film list).

The Britannia / Auto-Sky Drive-ins – ***Star Wars: A New Hope*** (1977). It wasn't called that then, just the first two words. They might as well have been "free marijuana" for the number of teens who lined up.

WHAT WAS THE WORST MOVIE YOU SAW AT EACH THEATRE?

The Elgin - ***Jinxed*** (1982). It was too. Star Bette Midler and director Don Siegel (uh...isn't that like giving Patti LuPone to John Woo?) allegedly fought the whole time. I did too—for a refund.

The Nelson - ***Inchon*** (1981). Laurence Olivier as Douglas MacArthur. I hope that casting director is still in the business. Can't wait for Judi Dench as Catwoman!

The Somerset - ***Return of the Jedi*** (1983) - Easy, nerds, easy! I know worse installments have since been made. But those Ewoks! Why wasn't it called *Alvin and The Chipmunks in Outer Space?*

The Rideau - ***Tidal Wave*** (1976). Actually, a Japanese cheapie made in 1973. Producer Roger Corman (a sign of quality), looking to cash in on the "disaster film" craze, bought it and inserted original footage of U.S. Ambassador Lorne Greene trying to clog a giant Japanese sink hole from his seat on the U.N. Hopefully, the hole swallowed the movie!

The Capitol Square - ***Clash of the Titans*** (1981) - Okay, not as bad as the 2010 remake, still...a *Downton Abbey*-worthy cast staging the world's dullest toga party.

The Place de Ville - ***Roadie*** (1980). A hopelessly wonky look at the lives of rock'n'roll roadies. I can see the producers scratching their heads after it flopped: "But we put Meatloaf together with Art Carney!"

The Towne / Bytowne Cinema – ***Crimes of Passion*** (1984). Okay, I went to see Kathleen Turner in promiscuous mode. I got what I paid for—but I also got Ken Russell, the man who makes Baz Luhrmann look like a tasteful conservative.

The Mayfair – ***Q the Serpent*** (1982) – Crap or camp, a question asked many a time at the B-movie loving Mayfair. And that title. Was it named after a cry by the assistant director? "Okay, guys —cue the serpent!"

The Elmdale – ***D.C. Cab*** (1983) – Who wouldn't back a high-concept premise like a ragtag taxi company trying to provide reliable service? Plus, that "all-star" cast: Max Gail, Gary Busey, and Mr. T. How much can I invest?

The St. Laurent – ***Carry On Girls*** (1973). The Carry On films —*Coronation Street* on Viagra. How I wish Brian De Palma had been brought into this fraternity. Imagine *Carrie On*.

The Phoenix – ***The Secret Policeman's Third Ball*** (1987) – By this, their third installment, the Amnesty International comedy and music benefits, once a hip, energetic showcase, had become sadly one-sided. The sponsors should have brought the editor responsible for brutalizing the comedy before a tribunal.

The Britannia / Auto-Sky Drive-ins – ***Hercules*** (1983). Bodybuilder Lou Ferrigno as the eponymous hero; you leave (early) convinced that Arnold Schwarzenegger and Jean-Claude Van Damme graduated from the Yale School of Drama.

OVERRATED AND UNDERRATED

NOW THAT I have you hooked, set your mind to these theatre-based inquiries—and prepare, as I'm doing, for debate...

WHAT WAS THE MOST UNDERRATED MOVIE YOU SAW AT EACH THEATRE?

The Elgin – ***Shoot the Moon*** (1982) – Memorable marital friction between Diane Keaton and Albert Finney. *Kramer vs Kramer* with cajones.

The Nelson – ***Outland*** (1980) – One of the best "elevator pitches" of all time: *High Noon* in outer space. With Sean Connery as the Sherriff no less (sadly, though, no Walter Brennan as chief cartographer).

The Somerset – ***The Cotton Club*** (1984) – Francis Ford Coppola's gangster-musical, recapturing the magic and danger of Harlem's most famous nightclub. I caught it on opening night and was stunned when the collective cries of "disappointment" came out. The musical numbers alone—what did those critics have in their ears: cotton?

The Rideau – ***Fingers*** (1978) – Harrowing cheapie asserting that New York City in the dirty Seventies could turn a man (Harvey

Keitel) into an animal. Based on the title, I thought I was in for a *Rocky*-style tale about bowling...

The Capitol Square – ***Melvin and Howard*** (1980) – A funny feel-bad from Jonathan Demme, about a quirky nobody claiming billionaire recluse Howard Hughes left him his fortune. The studio tried three different marketing campaigns; just like the hero, it's still waiting for its money.

Place de Ville – ***Rocky 2*** (1979) – Directed by Stallone yet almost as good as the first one, believe it or not. As for the subsequent entries, let's all sing: "Gonna cry nowwww..."

The Towne / Bytowne Cinema – ***The Green Room*** (1978) – Obscure Truffaut (it never even enjoyed mainstream release in Ottawa) about a man uber-obsessed with death. How much more commercial can you get?

The Mayfair – ***A Perfect Couple*** (1979) – Forgotten Robert Altman romcom that plays like *Marty* in modern-day L.A. Push zooms and multi-track overlapping not included.

The Elmdale – ***Cooley High*** (1976) – It was advertised as a black *American Graffiti* but this funny-feely look at African-American life in the early Sixties delivered so much more. Hmmm...how 'bout *Canadian Graffiti:* a greasy-haired Justin Bieber mooning cops at Portage and Main?

The St. Laurent – ***Moscow on the Hudson*** (1984) – Paul Mazursky's serio-comic look at the tribulations of immigrant life in NYC, starring Robin Williams as a Russian saxophone player. Guess Yakov Smirnoff had a gig in Branson.

The Phoenix – ***And the Ship Sails On*** (1983) – Fellini's last good film. *Titanic* on acid.

The Britannia / Auto-Sky Drive-ins – ***Sssssss*** (1973) – B grade horror flick about a man turning into a snake…and he doesn't sell computers. (Btw a back tire on the family car made the same sound as the title when we hit a large rock peeling out.)

WHAT WAS THE MOST OVERRATED MOVIE YOU SAW AT EACH THEATRE?

The Elgin – ***Top Gun*** (1986) – It put the "toxic" in "toxic masculinity."

The Nelson – ***The Omen*** (1976) – It was: four sequels and a remake.

The Somerset – ***The Towering Inferno*** (1974) – I got burned.

The Rideau – Uh, finding an overrated film at The Rideau would be like finding an Armani tux at Value Village.

The Capitol Square – ***Grease*** (1978) – Had anybody told me this Disney-fied version of the raunchy Broadway show would last through the ages I would have said, "Yeah, right! And what else —ABBA?!"

The Place de Ville – ***Star Trek: The Motion Picture*** (1979) – More like *Star Trek: The Motion to Adjourn*.

The Towne / Bytowne Cinema – ***Crouching Tiger, Hidden Dragon*** (2000) – Sorry but Bruce Lee didn't need guidewires to kick ass! (Suggestion for title for a B-grade remake: *Giant Tiger, Hidden Dragon*.)

The Mayfair – Worst thing I ever saw at The Mayfair: my ex with a hunky hockey player.

The Elmdale – ***Kramer vs. Kramer*** (1979) – *Shoot the Moon* without cajones (see the "underrated" list).

The St. Laurent – ***Dirty Dancing*** (1987) – Didn't bother to buy popcorn; there was more than enough corn on screen.

The Phoenix – ***Nosferatu the Vampyre*** (1979) – Werner Herzog riffing on the 1922 classic, with Klaus Kinski as the titular Transylvanian. Stinki Kinski.

The Britannia/Auto-Sky Drive-ins – ***Rambo*** (1985) – First blood, last money I ever spent on Stallone. (Btw shouldn't the Canadian release have been spelled *Rambeau*?)

FILMS WRITTEN BY DAN LALANDE

Portrait of the artist as a "movie juvie."

IN THE LATE 90'S, the independent film boom came to the nation's capital. Thanks to the homogenization of filmmaking technology, a hi-tech spawned investment pool, and a hungry international festival circuit, enterprising artists anywhere, including Ottawa, could produce a low-budget feature film which, potentially, could find an international audience, either in theatres or on television.

From 1998 to 2005, I was a seminal part of Distinct Features, an Ottawa-based independent production company which, after having cut its production teeth grinding out instructional films for government, techno interests, and charitable organizations, hopped on the indie movie bandwagon. Five feature films, written by (and occasionally co-starring) yours truly, were produced. You can catch them today on Canadian TV, your favourite streaming service or in foreign markets.

TWO'S A MOB (1998) – Written by (and co-starring) Dan Lalande and Rick Kaulbars. Who says showbiz doesn't make for strange bedfellows? Take, for instance, our lawyer, a Born-Again Christian, and his client, owner of a pornographic TV channel.

Together, they provided the modest financing for our first feature, a parody of mob films chronicling the comic adventures of a pair of contrasting brothers (and no, there's no pornography in it—unless you count our Seventies-set sight gag about a drive-by shooter-streaker). Little did we know that this 98-minute clothesline of jokes, written in a frenzied three days, was subscribing to the same premise as a big-budget Paramount production: *Mafia!* (universally deemed unfunny, it bombed) which cut our shot at distribution to the quick. Such are the risks of independent filmmaking! Still, *Two's A Mob* garnered good reviews from the few who saw it (it played a couple of local venues) and has found a home on Canadian television.

Kiss of Debt (2000) – Written by Dan Lalande and Derek Diorio. Starring Ernest Borgnine. The script, wherein a Preston Street restaurateur becomes romantically entangled with a Mafia kingpin's desperate daughter-in-law, was, for Ottawa, crazily ambitious; there were more storylines than you'd find in a Robert Altman or Richard Curtis film. In the end, not enough of it played. With the editor's help, it was trimmed to the central story. *Two's a Mob*, while liked by prospective distributors, was hindered by its lack of "marketable names." So, with what little, if generously provided, money we had, we went after Hollywood's histrionic marginalia, actors whose credits had grown sporadic. Enter the impossible-to-dislike Ernest Borgnine. He regaled us with anecdotes, set up cameras and lights, and, between takes, helped oblivious old ladies cross Somerset Street.

House of Luk (2001) – Written by (and co-starring) Dan Lalande. Starring Pat Morita and Michael Moriarty. The closest

Distinct Features came to attaining its goal: a splashy premiere (at Ottawa's Bytowne Cinema, though the film later played The Mayfair); a review in Variety (which called it both "poignant" and "over the top"); festivals in Toronto, Montreal, and Palm Springs; international sales. Pat Morita, star of this allegorical dramady, proved a handful (as you've read). Michael Moriarty, in a smaller part, proved just as difficult—though he did offer me one of the greatest compliments of my career. *Luk* was my first drama (prompted by the discovery that comedies rarely cracked film festivals). How had I fared, I wondered? The answer came the day he showed up on set. "You the guy who wrote this thing?" he asked in his friendly-scary rasp of his. "I understand you normally write comedy. Do the world a favour: keep writing drama."

House of Luk—star Pat Morita and author (with shaved head). CREDIT: Photo by Bev Chapell

Punch and Judy (2002) – Written by Dan Lalande. Starring Graham Greene and Pat McKenna. The hook: Joe Pesci meets Annie Hall (in this case, Pierre Brault, Ottawa theatre's one-man show king, and Brigitte Robinson, who, in the Eighties, had hosted the popular pre-teen TV show *Switchback*). It didn't play, quite, though the film boasted its quotient of street poetry, an attempt to capture some of the late night heart of Vanier or Hull onscreen. Fave moment: the climactic scene, when the titular couple (named after the famous battling puppets) have their make-or-break to and fro. Unseen to camera was me, on the floor, trying to suppress the pain of a sudden kidney stone attack. "Cut!" the director called after they had shot. Then, looking down at me: "How was that, Dan?" "Not bad," I grunted and groaned. "Can you get them to do one faster?" This was also the film on which we received a fateful phone call from the Voyageur bus station. "We have some film cans here," a voice loaded with mystery whispered. It was our rushes, freshly developed at a film lab in Montreal. "Looks like valuable stuff. If ya want it, it'll cost ya..." A police sting was set up in order to apprehend the blackmailers. Somehow, they got wise and never showed up. So, after going to our kindly investors on bended knee, a third of the picture had to be reshot.

A Taste of Jupiter (2005) – Written by Dan Lalande. Starring Eli Wallach and Teri Garr. A larger-than-life figure improbably enters the life of a lovesick librarian, his charm the solace she needs to negotiate a difficult personal circumstance. This piece of romantic-comic whimsy proved a little too grand for our production circumstances, not to mention my still developing drama chops. A discerning contributor to IMDB rightly wrote, "The script...flirts upon occasion with Magical Realism but is most effective through flashes of satire." Still, some of the film's poetic passages have their fans—as does the small, admirable catalogue produced, once upon a time, by Ottawa's Distinct Features.

A Taste of Jupiter star Eli Wallach and Dan Lalande. CREDIT: Photo by Bev Chapell

ABOUT THE AUTHOR

Photo by Rachel Gray

Dan Lalande is an Ottawa-based writer whose credits include household-name TV series' (*You Can't Do That on Television, The Raccoons, The Adventures of Teddy Ruxpin*), a published play (*Comeback*, with Robert Marinier), and five independent feature films, in which he has also appeared. In addition, Dan is an award-winning short story writer whose work has appeared in *Prairie Journal* and *The Spadina Literary Review*. He is also a contributor of film and book reviews to various publications and websites. When not writing, Dan stages classes in screen-based storytelling. While he has not shoplifted a movie-themed book in many years, he is bound to steal this one.

You can connect with Dan on Facebook and Twitter @Vizboy.

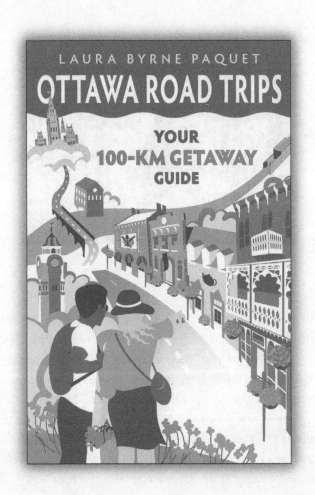